THE HUMAN MYSTERY
OF SEXUALITY

MARC ORAISON

THE
HUMAN MYSTERY
OF SEXUALITY

SHEED AND WARD * NEW YORK

© *Sheed and Ward, Inc., 1967*

This book was originally published in French under the title Le mystère humain de la sexualité. © *Editions du Seuil, 1966.*

Imprimatur: J.-Ch. Gallissaires, V. G.
Bordeaux, May 20, 1965

Library of Congress Catalog Card Number 67–13759

Manufactured in the United States of America

CONTENTS

v

Contents vii

THE HUMAN MYSTERY
OF SEXUALITY

I

THE FUNDAMENTAL
IMPORTANCE OF SEXUALITY

Introductory Paradox

No feast, celebration, or solemn occasion is really complete without the presence of flowers. Both the florist and his customers contribute considerably to human relations. And we have the assurance of the advertiser that to "say it with flowers" is so much better than to say it in person. Flowers, whether the orchids of the well-to-do or the poor man's violets, add something to the expression of thanks, the paying of respects, to the welcome and the good-bye, and to the apology. People honor the dead by placing flowers—even artificial flowers—over the coffin or about the tomb. And what would a wedding breakfast be, or even a meeting of the most serious learned society, if there were no flowers to grace the table?

Flowers have a language all their own. Experts in this language may appreciate the very fine shadings and the symbolism in each word, but who, for example, does not know that the lily carries the meaning of purity?

Man's outlook on this flower is vastly different from his view of, say, the cruder world of animals, and the difference—no matter how striking—is one written into the very nature of things. For flowers are the sexual organs of plants, and the world of flowers is a fair and delicate one. It is not the general form of the dahlia which men most admire; it is the very splendor of the plant, the flowers—the reproductive organs—which are so carefully cultivated and so proudly displayed in flower shows, for example. In the animal world, on the other hand, it is a dog's form and bearing, and not its sex, which men admire at an animal show.

On the human level, concealment of the reproductive organs from public view is a most basic element of civilization. Public exposure, accordingly, is regarded as of the utmost indecency. And yet, there is a strange ambivalence here, because successful clothes-designing, in far too many instances, rests on emphasizing the presence of what, in theory, ought be concealed. Extremely tight trousers and "falsies" will serve as adequate examples.

A moment's reflection thus reveals a very curious state

of affairs. Human reaction to that system of organs which transmits life is thoroughly ambivalent, and, the closer the approach to the center of this system, the more is this ambivalence emphasized. This is particularly observable in certain forms of sexual pathology, as verified by the findings of Freudian psychology. The behavior of the exhibitionist and of the Peeping Tom betrays this baffling mixture of the "desire to peek" and the "dread of being seen peeking."

Furthermore, simply to see or to be seen plays a role of rudimentary importance in the origin of this ambivalence. Only a human being can recognize himself in the mirror's reflection; only a human being looks at the flowers admiringly; and only a human being derives refined pleasure from the beauty of the flowers and personal satisfaction from his mysterious presence in the mirror. But what normal human being, apart from the professional horse trader or veterinarian, pays particular attention to the sex organs of the animal? Attention of this sort only further disturbs certain types of neurotics.

When men react in shame, their behavior is often so extreme as to betray what is obviously a fear. There are classic examples usually cited in this context, which most of us now regard as quite comical: the old practice by seminarians of using a stick to stuff the shirttails inside their trousers; wearing a pair of shorts while taking a bath or a shower. These customs evidence a prudery that has no foundation whatsoever in confessional belief—and, incidentally, such practices were by no means confined to Christian schools and seminaries. In fact, in some parts of the world the supposedly scientific language of anatomy is, at times, more emotion-charged than scientific: the arteries which supply the scrotum are still called "the shameful."

In this immediate connection, something else is to be observed. Whenever the two anecdotes of earlier seminarian life, mentioned above, are told, listeners never react with emotional indifference, with neutrality, so to speak; the listener either becomes indignant or else he indulges in a hearty laugh. And what does this mean? Simply that the individual's reaction is founded on some basic fear which calls for defensive action.

Literature itself bears the stamp of man's ambivalence regarding sexuality. In the writings of Rabelais, for example, sexuality is unmistakably present; in the works of the Countess of Segur, on the other hand, it is sexuality's very absence which is somehow present. It seems no exaggeration to say that every thought bears some relation to this most fundamental mystery of sexuality, whether that thought be one of pleasure in it, reflection upon it, or flight from it.

No human being can react to and adapt himself to his surrounding world except his behavior proceed elementally from his very real sexuality. The paradox is that this self-evident assertion has been so commonly misjudged, or kept under wraps, or so often the object of violent protest, as if it were the source of some incurable disease.

Today, however, we are witness to a profound change occurring throughout the world. Men are now convinced that scie... ...rce of a knowledge very much distinct fr... ...tained in philosophy and faith. ... ...which some trace back ... results.

M... ...of himself, of the wor... ...n presence in this wo... ...t, he has developed th... ...vity and by his own ... ...reflection. No longer ... ...ion and the symboliza- ... ...h as fundamental truths. ... ...beginnings in exact and ... ...rom there it advances to- ... ...e entirely free of precon-

... ...her philosophical or religious ... ...ts constitute a real revolu- ... ...l in man's customary way of living. ... ...hundred years, in particular, modern man ha... ...oped a decided need of self-acquired certitude before he will entertain teachings which, in times past, had been assumed as true beyond question. Despite appearances and the jeremiads of certain individual thinkers, this modern attitude is not necessarily man's declaration of independence from God. Even granted the possibility that scientific progress might lead to a denial of God, the fact of the matter is that the unrelenting march of science is precisely God's plan for man: the spiritualization of the universe. Far from causing a rupture in man's relations with his Creator, this new consciousness appears to be a giant step forward in man's dialogue with his God, a more satisfying answer to what God asks of man. It is inevitable that man will now have a keener and more vital realization of the tragedy of human unfulfillment whose resultant anguish seems, at times, unendurable. Never before, perhaps, has man so felt the need of salvation.

This new human situation calls for considerable purification in our thinking. Once it was discovered, for example, that thunder is an electrical phenomenon which can be measured, located and predicted, men no longer regarded it as the anger of God who lives in some imaginary "out there." The type of thinking which saw divine wrath in thunder accounts for some of the most acute tensions in today's world. And yet, astonishingly enough, today is witness to a growth in beliefs in the "magical" —astonishing, because it is taking place among leading scholars and intellectuals. The confusion between the marvelous and the supernatural—which science swore to dispel—is on the increase everywhere, and at a feverish rate. There are still some otherwise enlightened Catholics who adhere passionately to questionable apparitions, to supposed cases of mysticism, or to a particularly childish understanding of a miracle. And psychoanalysis is certainly a case in point when, even among a large number of general practitioners and specialists in medicine, there still remains an open and bitter anti-Freudianism. Were these people to make an honest effort to acquire a deeper understanding of modern psychiatry, instead of being always so eager to believe in "cures" and "miracles," they would see things differently. And, of course, we still have churchmen at sword's point with modern psychology—churchmen, by the way, who still cherish the most infantile beliefs regarding the devil ever to be found in the Middle Ages.

Modern science, for the most part, accepts this as rigid norm: God must no longer be confused with what is not God. Never before have Christ's words to the Samaritan woman carried more force: "There shall come a time when they will adore God in spirit and in truth."

All reflective thinking on sexuality must be exercised, therefore, within the context of this revolution in knowledge. For the first time in history, man has at his disposal completely new guidelines, and they have been developed by man alone. However, far from settling the basic questions, these guidelines and this new knowledge serve rather to make men more clearly and sharply aware of the existence and nature of the questions. We are completely baffled, for instance, to read what can only be called the childish prattlings of the great Leonardo da

Vinci on simple sexual physiology. His efforts to sketch, "in sections," the act of intercourse as well as his physiological explanation of an erection would be laughed at by today's high-school youngsters.

We must bear in mind that scientific findings in the field of sexuality are extremely recent. Physiology, properly so called, had scarcely begun before Claude Bernard, and clinical psychology really began with Freud.

Reflection on these new data, therefore, is the first requirement for a profitable study of sexuality. If we restrict this "mystery of sexuality" to the level of human knowledge, then divine revelation is bound to add to the fruits of our study—with this proviso, however, that divine revelation be itself freed, once and for all, of all superimposed and intolerable distortions and confusions.

Life and Sexuality

It may seem trite to say that sexuality is the very expression of life. But, trite or not, the statement bears a closer scrutiny.

What characterizes a living being, briefly, is that it has something essentially distinct from matter, something which, by itself, assures that being's stability in action and in reaction to its environment. The pebble rests on the ground; the grass "sucks at" the pebble. The commonplace saying has it that the cattle eats the grass, then man eats the cattle, and, after that, man sits down to think. Trite though all this may seem, a great deal remains to be learned from pondering these simple truths.

In a certain sense, the struggle begins with the very first appearance of life. True, struggle may not be the most precise word: the ground cannot accurately be said to "defend itself" against the pebble, for the inertia of matter is inertia, and nothing else. However, the individual living being is in constant affinity with other living beings, so that attack and defense become the basic law of life. All branches of zoology give us a good idea of just what takes place in the world of life, and we need only turn to the motion-picture popularizations of zoology to see this fundamental law of life in all its vividness. Frequently what we see strikes us as the utmost cruelty.

Just what is at stake in this struggle of life? Quite obviously, continuance in existence, survival in time: in other words, a victory over that dimension of the world which is revealed in the struggle—the dimension called time. Not time in the psychological sense, by any means, but time in the sense of succeeding and dynamic unfoldings of real beings, time as the measure of change. In non-living beings, this dimension of time is not easily observable, and the resultant illusion is that non-living beings do not change. It takes thousands of years for a mountain to be worn away, and it is all but impossible for us to imagine, for example, what the Grand Canyon looked like thousands of years ago.

Life is duration in a new form and begins with the individual. That individual is responsible for his life and it
is incumbent on him to see that it continues. Why? And
what does all this mean? A fundamental and absolutely
inescapable question is involved here, a question to which
science, as such, is unable to provide an answer. For the
fact of the matter is that life is not satisfied with mere
continuance; it seeks its own expansion. Within every
living being there throbs that internal dynamism which is
bent on self-expression, on self-development, on self-com-
pletion. The struggle is not really, therefore, a struggle for
existence so much as for ever more existence. The modi-
fications of this inner dynamism are clearly of an infinite
variety. Life's outcome is never more than relative; in
other words, life in general reaches out toward a permanent state, one that is unattainable and always insecure.

Growth naturally brings to the individual both facility
in action and a certain fullness of being. At that stage
the struggle for existence begins and the aging process
itself sets in even as life initiates its course. Regarded in
his isolation, the individual enjoys a shortlived conquest of
the passing of time, a rough effort, at best, which is cal-
culated to bring on failure. However, there is a certain
amount of satisfaction in the more enduring victory of the
species of which the individual is part. A dog lives for,
say, fifteen years, but after thousands and thousands of
years the canine species is still very much with us. Sex-

uality is found at this level of the continuity of the species. Each individual shares in this to his own proper degree by reason of a persistent drive which goes beyond his actual dimensions and limits. The individual member is caught up in this overwhelming dynamism of his species, affected by an expansion that is beyond him.

In the very early stages of individual life—vegetal or animal life—the sexual apparatus, properly so called, begins to develop. This development, in the animal series, starts with certain protozoan types, is already outlined in the heliozoans, and is unmistakably present in the foraminifers.

Nature seems to take delight in its experimental research to discover the best possible solution. The reproductive methods of some races are so complex to us who observe them as to verge on the bizarre. Save for the rare exception, however, the universal principle is the specific distinction between two classes of individuals—male and female. This is unquestionably the predominant theme: in the evolving sexual organization, the separation of the species into two is what allows their absolutely unique union of copulation, the creative cause of life. And the more perfect living beings are, the clearer is the meaning of this arrangement: for the perpetuation of life, there must be two individuals who are similar but, at the same time, radically different by their very sexuality. At certain periods in their life-rhythm, they are drawn together in a union that is both intense and brief, one that results in

fecundation. This general and absolutely basic biological
reality seems, at first glance, quite simple. On reflection,
however, nothing is more inexplicable than this deep-
seated law of nature: for the perpetuity and growth of the
species, sexed individuals in this species must seek something outside themselves. They become obsessed by desire for sexual copulation in order to maintain a collective
existence that goes infinitely beyond the life of the individual. In living nature, this is the rudimentary biological meaning of sex. In the eyes of science—and this must
be candidly admitted—the ultimate meaning of the sexual
fact remains hermetically sealed in obscurity.

Sexuality and Death

Another finding, however, seems even more disturbing.
In order for the amoeba to reproduce itself, it must split
in two, following the process of scissiparity. This means
that the "mother amoeba" becomes two "amoeba daugh-
ters," and that, following reproduction, it has surrendered
its existence as a distinct individual.

As soon as the sexual organization make its appearance
—and by this is meant the structuration, however ele-
mentary, of a distinct reproductive apparatus in individuals of a species—the process is reversed. The sexed
individual now continues in existence without dependence on its reproductive activity. And it is on this level

that there appears the inescapable death of the individual. The amoeba, splitting in two, does not die. Male and female dogs, reproducing by their union, die at the end of a certain time, insofar as they are distinct individuals. There is a curious paradox involved here: wherever that which causes perpetuity of life—the life, that is, of the species—appears as something distinct (the reproductive apparatus), death is revealed as the lot of the individual.

Almost immediately the dynamism responsible for the perpetuity and expansion of the species shows an ever more noticeable stability of the individual as such. The individual no longer splits into two new individuals; rather, the species divides into individuals that are, in some way, more "definitive." It is at this point that the intense activity involved in sexual union reveals, as it were, obsession for a new "unity." And it is precisely here that there appears the irremediable weakness of the individual in his own separate existence.

In summary, the specific and increasingly complex refinement of the "life function" is also the very occasion on which mortality of the individual reveals itself. No one can be indifferent to what reflection on this fact discloses.

The Questioning Consciousness

Man is a living being among other living beings, yet of a radically different kind. In the light of modern science we may say that he is a product of evolution, yet of a wholly different kind of being from the universe whence he took origin. As disclosed in his bodily structure, this difference lies in the remarkable growth of his brain. Man's cerebral network is so complex that it is impossible to predict with any certainty just how he will react to the surrounding world.

Perhaps the most felicitous expression of this real existential upheaval can be found in *Les Animaux dénaturés* of Vercors wherein one of the characters points out that man wears charms, whereas animals do not. This very novel distinction serves as an undisputed guidepost because it means, in short, that, when his questions are not settled, man makes up his own answers. His answers are imaginative, magical, always symbolic, yet in their own way they express ineffable, deep realities, even strikingly deep intuitions. Much later on, science or something else will corroborate such intuitions.

For thousands of years before man heard, with Abraham, the voice of Him who is, man conjured up a multiplicity of his own gods. Even now, man continues his search for imaginary gods. True, he is not aware that this is the nature of his search, but he is actually reverting to magic and he does distort divine revelation. In light of this, for example, Freud was able to trace the origin of the Oedipus myth to the darkest recesses of man's consciousness.

Now, if man devises his own answers, it is only because

he raises questions. The animal is alive, but it is man who questions and knows that he, in turn, is being questioned His relation to the world is not the same: he is not just a component part of it; the world is outside man and, *at the same time,* he stands before it, probing it with questions. He is really "taken out of nature," as Vercors sees it. This means, in a sense, that man is uprooted from that very nature of which he is, nevertheless, the most refined expression—and this by what we must call a transcendental "vocation." Contemporary thought is, perhaps, characterized by the fact that the interrogating, dynamic character of consciousness is more fundamental than its reflective character; in fact, it is the very wellspring of reflection.

Our modern world, particularly during the past ten years, is fundamentally the world of history. Twentieth-century man is wholly engrossed in the most exacting possible search into his beginnings, and that on both the collective plane of pre-history and in the social and individual sphere of psychoanalysis. The human race has never before been so concerned about painstakingly exploring its origins. Up until modern times it was known that we "came from God." Now there is a further question: *How?* This query is linked up with man's struggle for knowledge. Worth emphasizing, in season and out, is the truth that this question is itself the reply given to man's vocation as it was determined by God the Creator.

The essence of the question which man, as a person,

raises from the very first moment of his life may be stated in a deceptively simple form: "Who am I?" The answer to this involves the exploration, impossible of completion, of the boundless network of relations which man establishes with all about him, both the human and non-human world. An eighty-year old man has not yet fully answered this simple question regarding his identity; he has not completed self-discovery. At eighty-one years of age, he will doubtlessly live through situations which he has never before experienced and from which (if he does not shut off interior reflection) he will be able still further to sift hitherto unknown elements of self-knowledge. Yet, from the moment of his birth, this same man—inarticulately, of course—has been asking this very same question.

Consequent upon Freudian discoveries, one entire period of man's personal history, namely, his hitherto unexplored early childhood, has become part and parcel of scientific knowledge. It takes only a moment's thought to realize that a gulf separates a puppy after sucking and a month-old baby after his nursing. The baby looks at his mother, and its very glance is a silent question, a searching after a "reference-situation," a truly ambivalent effort of separation and return. Between the mother and her nursing child there springs up an intense dialogue, a whole world of activity which no language can translate.

Regardless, on this emotional level which precedes explicit knowledge, the baby's first months are occupied

with the rudimentary search for its identity. First victory crowns this search at the moment when the infant is about to recognize itself clearly in a mirror. The infant itself will, as it were, "coincide" with the image of his unconscious self (which he has already worked out) and with the image which he sees before him. Understandably, then, Dr. Lacan and his school of psychoanalysis stresses this "mirror stage."

The search for identity—this "Who am I?"—is conducted in a life of sexual differentiation. Freud's fundamental teaching holds that the individual begins to question his own presence in the world from the position that it is a boy or a girl, and this perspective dominates the entire search. While the sexual reality does not create the specific nature of human consciousness, it does serve as a basic, essential condition for the direction which developing consciousness takes.

When all of this was stated in clear and forthright formulation at the end of the last century, why were there such loud and indignant protests? And the hue and cry may still be heard from certain schools of thought. It becomes particularly hard to understand in view of the fact that Freudian psychology has been on a course of steady progress in changing and advancing psychiatry, modern theories of education, the study of human relations and other related fields.

No one need ever again have the slightest fear in view of the fact that the sexual mystery has been uncovered

and shown to be an essential fact of life. For today we realize that anatomical and biological differentiation is the essential vector of all emotional evolving through which the child will gradually achieve self-awareness all the way up to the spiritual level. No human being may say "I" except in functional dependence on his sexuality, whether he accepts this truth or not.

There is no reason for surprise here. After all, sexual organization in living beings is revealed with progressive distinctness all along the scale of beings and in function of their progressive complexity. This dehiscence of the species, which allows, strictly speaking, for sexual attraction in all its power (but also its relativity) is now known to have its special mode of being, on the human level, in a questioning consciousness. But this notion must be understood in its fullness to include not merely clear consciousness and reflection, but also the pre-consciousness which characterizes the earliest stages of the child's life.

The Separation

Here language comes to grief and shows its inadequacy. We can speak of what the child feels only in terms of what adults think. Although this vocabulary has the virtue of clarity, it has the distinct disadvantage of petrifying, so to speak, of compartmentalizing and of

oversimplifying what, as lived, is infinitely complex. Accordingly, despite the handicaps and in order to overcome continuing ignorance about the very foundations of the dynamic personality, we must use the language and vocabulary at our disposal, never losing sight of the fact that this language has only symbolic value and can merely suggest a world which, in itself, is inexpressible. In our explanations, then, the vocabulary must not be taken literally; rather, continual effort should be made to go beyond articulation of these phenomena to understand what actually is in question.

Given this precaution, we can point out that the central theme of the child's first experience is that of the *cutting*, or separation. Obviously, when a child is ready to be born, it must be cut away from something, from a "world which is not itself." This sounds perfectly self-evident, but it is really a very complex concept brimming with meaning.

This particular kind of being which comes into existence is intrinsically bound up with the sexed transmission of life. Not merely a life-experience proper to the child, it is, moreover, something lived in the child's relationship with its mother and, therefore, something experienced in the life of the mother herself.

It must be stressed, in connection with the clearly visible episode of the cutting of the cord, that the separation occurs on two very different levels. At first glance, it

appears that this cutting away is effected only on the
visible level. By the action of the scissors, some short
distance from the navel, the child appears to be cut away
directly from its mother. Actually, however, as a result of
this operation the baby is separated only from the closed
"interior world" of the amniotic sac in which it has lived
up to that point. The true cutting-away of child from the
mother occurs in the separation between the uterus and
the ovum. The separation of the placenta and the delivery
of the child are the effective separation between the
world of the mother and the world of the child. However,
the baby does not live through this experience in the
same way as the mother. The baby experiences the cutting-away as a rude eviction from a closed environment,
which was its own, and as the beginning of an autonomy
which, in a matter of seconds, will demand considerable
effort for survival. In a sense, therefore, to be born means
to be separated, to lose something, to break out of a
shadowy world which must be relinquished due to an
irresistible force.

Too seldom is stress placed on this aspect of "inaugural
loss," but depth psychology shows its importance and
emphasizes how human existence begins with a truly
dramatic event. Present at the very outset of human existence is something akin to homesickness.

Continuing its explanation of this very early stage in
the child's life, modern psychology emphasizes the child's
difficulty in working out the relation with the object that

is not itself, but which is important for the child for the twofold reason that the object is not the child and that the object invites the baby to possess or reject it.

This first "object" is the mother's breast or its equivalent, the nursing bottle; that is to say, the first object of desire at this stage is essentially oral. Here again, the separation has two meanings: for the child in its first months, separation means the experiencing of the mother and the breast which is the "object for the baby" and in some way "detachable"; for the mother, however, the separation is an experience between her breast and the baby. It is really no paradox that our very first experience of the relation to another, by which we find ourselves, is inexorably stamped by doubt and "misunderstanding." Furthermore, it is not surprising that the same ambiguity continues in the adult's unconscious emotional state in different degrees, in his relations in life.

Pathology expresses here the consequences—granted, extreme consequences—of this basic "misunderstanding": the schizophrenic who has become part of his mother's life as "her very own sex object," something about which she, in her own childhood, had been incurably frustrated.

Only periodically, however, does the baby possess the object desired, its mother's breast, nor does it always get what it wants, precisely when it wants it. In this area of unavoidable frustration the baby gets its first picture of self, of the object which is outside it. The baby is able, too, in one way or other, to form an image of its relationships with the object. These relations constitute, as it were, the unconscious outlines of the psychic life which psychoanalysts are exactly right in calling the "world of phantasies." The baby's life has not yet developed to the level of imagination properly so called.

Alternate frustrations, then weaning; the small child learns to react in accordance with whatever separates him from the object of his desire. But the very object of his desire is never, fundamentally, what he lacks. There is a basic want of proportion between "the object of desire," in general, and the precise object desired at present. Because of the sexual way in which life is transmitted, subjective human experience must be characterized only by dissatisfaction from the very outset. Even on very different levels, man will never find anything but a substitute for his desire, something which gives passing satisfaction, but which, by virtue of its very inadequacy, continues to arouse a perpetual search for something more satisfying. Of all the different forms of desire, sexual desire, properly so called, is perhaps most noted for this trait of ambiguity.

Very early, and in this context, whether a child is a boy or a girl has enormous significance before that child is able to become conscious of its self in its experienced relations. In short, the difference between a boy and girl in the first years depends on whether there is or is not an exterior object. The genital area is equipped with particular sensitivity and a specialized system of nerves, and this condition quickly assumes a leading role in the child's formation of its image, one based on the senses and emotions. This structuration is a complex and obscure world, as modern psychoanalytic study has made clear from its investigations, but certain aspects of it must be studied toward understanding their importance.

Up to a certain point in his development, the young boy, for example, can regard every other human being who comes near him as only a fairly representative picture of himself. He is unable to conceive of another person who does not have this "object" as something essential to his sense-exploration of himself. He can picture his mother, along with other persons, only according to this type. In the phantasmal life of the small child lies the full importance of what psychoanalysts call the "phallic mother." The problem comes alive for the child at that moment when he discovers, much earlier than is ordinarily believed, the difference between the sexes. If the little boy could phrase his problem in symbolic terms, he would ask, "How can anyone live without that? Can a person lose it? Can he be separated from it?" At this juncture in the young boy's life, his questions meaningfully reveal the fear of castration, a fear aroused by conflicts of opposition with adults.

The little girl's experience takes an opposite tack, and her thoughts would be expressed somewhat like this: "But why don't I have this 'object'? What I do have—is it less important than the 'object'? Or was this 'object' taken away from me as a punishment?"

It is no exaggeration to say that, at this very tender age,

the small child organizes his "rational coming to consciousness" around the presence or absence of this "object" (so important because it represents the only difference) and around the uneasiness attendant on its loss or absence.

Despite the scant attention given to this subject, it should be immediately evident that this "castration" theme is present, and to a very considerable extent, in the obscure areas of human psychology: jokes, analogies, the more or less off-color allusions, the all too common threats in training the child ("If you aren't a good boy, I'll take that away from you.") which confirm this fact are everyday occurrences. Threatening children is certainly no way to help them to a full personality. We may never know how many people come to the consultation rooms of psychotherapists because they are mired in inhibitions and uneasiness connected with the quite extra-sexual expressions of their personality—and all because of parental threatenings in their early childhood.

The following anecdote, told to me by the family itself, will give some notion of the deep-seated character of this uneasiness with respect to the sexual object.

The child in this case, five or six years old, attended a nearby kindergarten conducted by religious women. One evening he came home, visibly excited by a whole new world of ideas. After a moment he confided, "You know something, mother? Today I learned how God created the world!"

"Oh, yes? And how did God do it?"

"Oh, he began by creating Adam. And then he was afraid that Adam would be bored. So, he put him to sleep and took out one of his ribs to make Eve. Only—and here's the point—God didn't take enough from Adam. So he had no way to make a little faucet for Eve. But that was all right because Eve—well, she had a lot of hair. So, God took a handful of it and put it on her so she wouldn't notice the difference."

This whole topic of the "separation" is of crucial importance and has an essential connection with the reproduction of life. In this sense, sexuality can be said to condition the whole of existence on every level of development. To develop "self-being" as a distinct consciousness, it is necessary to be "cut off" from another. In the case at hand, it is being "cut off" from the mother, who, in turn, is mother only in a completely distinct and profound relation to the "other" of the father. Now, then, both the mother and father began life in this world by being "cut off" from their respective mothers, and those mothers—and so *ad infinitum*. It is almost dizzying to ponder this transmission of experience. And the meaning beneath all this is, purely and simply: one can encounter the "other" only if he be "cut off" and become a distinct person.

In a word, according to modern psychology, the first experiences of a child's life enable that child so to integrate this "separation (from the mother) to which he

owes his existence" as to acquire a consciousness of itself
that is both satisfying for and adequate to the child's own
sexual condition, that is, the condition of being a boy or
a girl. As a consequence of this separation, he or she will
be able, later on, to participate in the very complex interpersonal relations of existence, and to do so without
formless fears, obsessive apprehensions and rampant aggressiveness. Too, this separation will make it possible
for the child to endure the fundamental and mysterious
"misunderstanding" of human existence and then go on
to search out life's meaning.

It next becomes absolutely essential that the child terminate that period of its life in which it is, first, the
sexual object of the mother and, secondly, of the father.
The young girl must integrate the very absence of phallus
as her own positive reality, as her own proper possession.
She will achieve this integration by resolving her "castration anguish." In his turn, the young boy must achieve
his own integration, and he is well on the way when his
sex is integrated as part of him rather than as a separate
object obsessing him with primitive phantasies, and when
he can do this without fear of losing it in his opposition
to adults—his father, in particular.

Two pathological cases may help to illustrate the importance of this castration theme.

A young man, no more than twenty years of age, has
literally focused all his affective attention on one of his
male friends. Despite all his efforts to change this state

of affairs, he is haunted by an overpowering urge to see his friend in the nude. His desire is a powerful mixture of fear and sexual excitement. The object of his desire is complete nudity, but, when the elements of that desire are broken down, what he really wants is to see his friend's phallus fully exposed. Yet, the fact is that every-time he does have the chance to see his friend in the nude, as during common showers at the club, all desire and its attendant sexual excitement disappear at once. Analysis, over a period of time, has enabled this young man to realize that he was not really eager to see his friend's phallus. Actually, his search centered around a phantasmal (in the psychological meaning of the word), imaginary phallus which *did not exist* and which obsessed him by its very absence: *the maternal phallus*. The serious neurosis of this young man's mother never permitted him to integrate this particular aspect of the fundamental theme of castration. In this case, as in others, the results of exclusively analytic therapy verified, beyond any possible doubt, the origin of his troubles. After three years of treatment, his obsessional "quest" disappeared, and the young man became quite normal.

The second case is that of a woman whose life was one long, intense suffering. Like the rest of us, she had good qualities and bad. In some ways, she was extremely feminine, a "seductive" type. In her professional life, in particular, she went out of her way to overpower and dominate men. A genuinely unbearable person, she suffered from continual dissatisfaction, and with no relief in sight. From the very beginning of her childhood, this young woman had never been able to integrate her feminine makeup into the decidedly disturbed network of family relations. In her emotional life—unconsciously, of course—she was completely incapable of tolerating the absence of the phallus, and she felt this lack as a castration. Her life was a constant shuttling between artificial femininity and masculine vindictiveness; she was utterly disagreeable and viciously overbearing toward everyone: toward women because they had no phallus; toward men because they had one.

Anguish

In everyday language, "anguish" is used to express many things, and, therefore, it expresses nothing accurately. The word is used to cover every type of vague fear, apprehension and anxiety, a certain amount of emphasis being generally placed on nervous, bodily emotion.

Despite the cryptic, oracular sound of the word, Dr. Lacan seems to explain it better than most when he says that anguish arises when the support of a defect fails. A simple example may clarify this somewhat.

Suppose I have some business to conduct or a serious problem I have to discuss with someone. Now imagine that I find myself "glued" to this someone, nose to nose, shoulder to shoulder. I am gripped by an uneasiness that I can't explain. I no longer *distinguish* his existence from my own. I no longer know *where* I am; still worse, I don't know very well *who* I am. It may even be said that I am no longer certain about *whether* I exist (although I must know that I do, because I am in doubt). However, the moment I stand back and see that between this someone and myself there intervenes *empty space, a no-man's land, a separation,* then I recover at once a comforting consciousness of myself as being present. The "uneasiness" disappears.

Anguish is found on the level of this uneasiness. Entirely different from the threat of death, anguish corresponds, so to speak, to the risk of being "absorbed," of becoming reincarnated as an object that loses not existence, but existence as something *distinct.* The experience of anguish enters the content of daily life, and yet its full, true meaning defies language to express it. All of us, at one time or other, find ourselves in company with a person who makes us ill at ease, so we try to cut the meeting short. We need room to breathe. This can be explained by the concept of anguish as we have described it. In the presence of such a person, my worry is centered on the threat that the distance between us will disappear, and this can become unbearable.

Psychoanalytic probing has disclosed that one of the baby's first reactions is, in rational terms—therefore fundamentally inadequate terms—the desire to return to the mother's womb. Unquestionably, this "homesickness" for the intra-uterine life which the baby has just abandoned —and quite violently—is a characteristic of the baby's first real experience.

As soon as he is forced out, "cut off from his root," the child finds himself *present* to his mother. At a very early stage, the mother is *the other* in the eyes of her baby, even though the baby is not fully aware that he is no longer part of her. As far as the baby is concerned, to return to its mother's womb would be the same as to become part of the body of the other. This would mean the disappearance of the "distance" which the separation brought about and which is the very first, though confused, perception of self. In other words, the desire to return to the mother's womb arouses anguish in a very real sense.

This fundamental ambivalence is what constitutes, to some extent, the very dynamism of the evolving emotional personality. Of course—and I do not think that repetition of this caution is pointless—this abstract type of description is inadequate at best, but it must suffice to allow us a glimpse of meaning.

The language difficulty aside, we must admit that the infant, from the moment of its birth, is held in the grip of anguish such as we have described anguish. The infant will continue to find escape from it while, at the same time, it seeks to realize its yearning for "the mother's womb" with a view to the future and not to the past, and this—on a level that becomes more and more symbolic—along the lines of what may accurately be called "sublimation."

This entire phenomenon is carried through all the child's personal activities, both those which are strictly speaking, sexual (the note of "return to the uterus" having wholly changed the meaning of this term) and all those activities by which the subject becomes integrated into the social community. This community, itself, is always tinged with a maternal "note," and we notice it in such expressions as "mother country" and "holy mother the Church."

Two case histories may shed some light on the matter. The cases deal with two nineteen-year-old boys from vastly different backgrounds. At first glance, their histories seem to have no point in common.

No sickness was involved in the first case. Because of his childhood and his first years of adolescence, he showed evident symptoms of difficulty in self-development. However, his problem was resolved in a normal way because he was able to establish a network of satisfying interhuman relations. In common parlance, the young man had been "asocial" or "delinquent." In his confrontation with organized society, his attitude had been very ambivalent, resulting in both aggressive and shy expressions. On the one hand, the young man was decidedly afraid to be "denied" in his own singularity by permitting himself to become integrated in society; at the

same time, there was unmistakable evidence of deep
homesickness and a resentment against those who, he felt,
were conspiring to block normal integration in the course
of his development. At certain times, his very appearance
gave exact expression to the anguish (as we have defined
it) from which he was fleeing. His entire problem resolved
itself to this: the desire to assume his place within the
"bosom of society" and the insurmountable anguish which
this very desire caused in him. His problem had its roots
in his relations with a very neurotic and possessive mother
who treated him, in his own words, "as a doll, or as her
kitten."

His case history brought out that this particular young
man had lived in a nursery during his first two or three
years. His earliest relations with his "nursery mother" had
been just about normal. However, when he came back to
live with his natural mother, he was not yet sufficiently
grounded, and the possessiveness of his real mother
aroused real anguish in him. Had he lived with her from
the very outset, more than likely he would have become
a serious neurotic. Undoubtedly, the young man was
spared this fate by the fact that the first two or three
years had contributed to his escape from a very primitive
regression. In relation to his mother, to society and to
women in general, this young man had long maintained
the same ambivalent reflex attitude he displayed while
still under the domination of anguish. When he made the
acquaintance of a mixed group of men and women, mar-

ried and single, a new dialogue began. By common agreement, he and a forty-five-year-old man struck up a father-son relationship, something which he had evidently never had. In this way, he was able to resolve his "interior struggle" (the expression is his) and to bring about its sublimation. In a casual, yet meaningful way, the young man declared the end of his struggle when he mentioned to his adoptive father, "Yesterday I was happy. I realized then that you did not need me."

The case history of the second boy is very different. At the age of nineteen, he committed suicide. His family, traditionally middle-class in the good sense of that expression, had undergone particularly severe hardships overseas during World War II, and these difficult years unfortunately coincided with his birth and earliest childhood. To make matters worse, the young man's mother had undergone rather serious surgery when he was but a few months old.

One morning the young man was found dead in his room. He had swallowed a strong dose of quick-acting poison. The long letter which he had left behind, although very coherent, shook his family as incredible. He had no apparent reason for what he had done. He had been getting along well in his studies, had many fine friends, and there had been no broken love affair in his young life. His suicide, he wrote, was a "philosophical one": life's absurdity; existence without meaning; his inability to face life.

Regarded from a psychoanalytic perspective, however, the young man's action took on meaning in the light of his behavior toward his mother. He had caused her untold alarm for a number of years, and, because she had found him "nervous," she asked him to see a psychologist. Sometimes he would show a thoroughly puerile need of affection; at other times, a kind of inexplicable fright seemed to possess him. He would shove his mother away, as if terrified, when she leaned over to embrace him while saying goodnight. In seeking some connection between these symptoms and the dramatic circumstances of his childhood, psychologists concluded that the young man had never begun to resolve the primitive ambivalence, that is, the anguish involved in the desire to return to the womb.

Masculinity, Femininity

Existence in this world is possible only according to one's sexual differentiation and according to the manner in which this has been integrated into the image of one's self, dating from pre-conscious foundations. Therefore, there is a masculine presence before the world and a feminine presence before the world. Human consciousness can only be sexed, that is, the working out of a dialogue in the very large sense, of which, all things considered, the most surprising element is that it is so often

involved in conflict, even in the most advanced successes
of love. The immediate future will not see a civilization
in which women and men will have found both their
respective and reciprocal places in a definitive and wholly
satisfying way.

If, in the case of the child, the possession or not of the
anatomical phallus has a primordial importance, it is perfectly clear that, on the level of adult psychology, the
"phallic function" is of the imaginative or symbolic order.
For example, a domineering woman is said to "wear the
trousers," which means, in blunt terms, that she is the
man, that she is the one who "has the phallus." We must
conclude, therefore, that what specifies personality is, to
some degree, the presence or absence of this phallic object—whether it be real, imaginary, or symbolic.

Man possesses his own specific attribute as an object
which is exterior, explorable, and, we may almost say,
capable of being considered as really apart from him.
Many reactions of this object are beyond his voluntary
control, but he certainly knows this, and it places him in
a position of initiative. In the sexual encounter, it is he
who *penetrates* (and this term is to be understood on different levels of symbolic signification), and it is he who
projects, who *gives*. In his own existence, the male is
really the one who is less dependent on his emotional life:
he meets situations head-on and plunges into them with
initiative; he investigates reality and seeks to find its
contours, its simple and precise structure; he prefers clear,

well organized ideas and judgments which permit him to act; and, although he knows how to impose his will, he does, at the same time, give what he has to offer.

The woman possesses her sexuality in a manner which is much more mysterious. Her own "object," which corresponds, so to speak, to "the absence of the accessible object," is completely within her interior and is unexplorable. The one- or two-year-old boy who plays with himself is exploring something; the little girl, on her part, is exploring nothing, or a "non-something." Actually, however, the woman is physiologically much more "impregnated" with her sexuality, both with regard to visceral and anatomical relations and by hormonal interactions. And her physical structure, in the sexual encounter, leads her to be "forced in her secret," to *receive*.

There is too much erroneous talk about feminine "passivity." The term is ambiguous, to say the least. A woman's attitude should not be set in opposition to activity as to a contrary; rather, the question should concern another form of activity, one that is very positive. It would be much more accurate and becoming to speak of "receptivity," and receptivity is quite as active as initiative. Would one have meaning without the other?

In the great general dialogue between the sexes which, on its own level, expresses in a sharp but incomplete way the "sexual dialogue" properly so-called, man and woman ask and give, both of them; clearly, however, the asking

and the giving is not the *same* thing for the man as for
the woman.

The woman is the one, existentially, who will be much
more dependent on emotional life, even though she cannot determine its precise and logical limits. The woman
receives in welcome more than she offers. She is the one
who "develops the secret" without knowing precisely
what she is developing in the deepest recesses of her soul.
It is she who "feels" beyond the limits of rational exploration, with both the experienced certitude and the simul-
taneous lack of precision which this entails. It is the
woman at every level, and not merely at the genital level,
who offers herself, receives, develops, and finally produces what the man cannot produce alone and what she
could never produce without him: *life*.

Unfulfillment

What has been said here is simply the expression of gen-
eralities with which everybody would be in nearly full
agreement. However, once our consideration centers on
the real as lived, things are no longer so simple or so
clear. Actually, no man is fully, exclusively, and defini-
tively completed in his existential masculinity; no woman
in her femininity.

The identification game of the first years is very com-

plex. Just as embryonic remnants of the other sex continue to exist in every individual, so, too, the individual
psychic constitution preserves "dynamic traces" of the
primitive conflicts which psychoanalysis has been able to
reveal. In Paul Clandel's *Satin Slipper,* Camille tells
Prouheze that there is something of the woman in her.

Personality development is open to psychoanalytic investigation. Accordingly, it becomes clear that this dynamism, in an emotional and relational history that is in
each instance unique, is directed toward total integration
of sexuality. But it is equally clear that no one arrives
there completely. Putting it another way, we can conjure
up for ourselves an idea of the ideal Man and of the ideal
Woman. But, at the same time, we see that they do not
exist, that "they are nobody."

The relationship of equal to equal in perfectly per-
ceived complementarity never exists in the pure state,
that is, as fully constituted. Vagueness and tension are
what remain, no matter what relationship may have been
established, whether it be the relation of a gentleman to
a saleslady or of a lady customer to her grocer.

Perhaps the man most obviously certain of his virility
(and not in a narrow and genital-sexual meaning of the
word) is the one who unconsciously shudders before the
image of a threatening mother or an unapproachable
father and who actually more than makes up for this fear.
Every human being is conscious or unconscious of a lack
of certitude or security along the line of his complete sex-

ualization. From the modern, psychological perspective, none of us corresponds fully and exclusively with his proper sex any more than he does so on the physiological level. The gaps between real and psychological sex are sometimes astonishingly dramatic. The case of transvestism is a particularly clear example. Why is it that a twenty-five-year-old butcher, solidly built and strikingly masculine in physique, experiences no sexual desire, but is continually obsessed by an almost unbearable uneasiness when he cannot dress as a woman?

This pathological case, however, is only a caricature of a fundamental human reality. In a word, this utterly essential question of "Who am I?" (raised by and in sexuality) is never completely settled. The light of modern psychology and modern medicine illumines the truth that there is no clear boundary between the "normal" and the pathological. Rather, there is the rough and hasty or gradual disclosure of the conflict that is, to some degree, part of the person's make-up. What is more normal, and yet more pathological, than disease and death?

This viewpoint, however (invariably subject of dispute), leads us away from sexuality as such. In the area of sexuality, the question seems to enjoy sharper focus. There is nothing astonishing about this, because sexuality is the fundamental fact of life and the essential way by which the human arrives at spiritual consciousness.

This "insecurity of sexualization" is not the least mystery. In individual case histories, investigated by psycho-

analysis, the labyrinthine path of events can evidently be
followed or traced back to their origin. But a question of
a quite different order is not thereby answered: "How did
things happen to get this way?"

The more life is refined and perfected, the more it is
perpetuated by way of sexuality. The sexual reality rotates
between separation, coming together, and being cut off,
and all this places man in an alternation of anguish and
encounter, an alternation which is, in the final analysis,
itself incapable of any form of perfectly clear solution. In
its manifestations that are directly sexual (in the ordinary
sense of the word), as well as in the general outlook of the
person, sexuality is the privileged precinct of the consciousness of the "separation which brings about [per-
sonal] existence" and of the ambiguity in man's relations
to others.

At bottom, such is the most troublesome conclusion of
the findings of modern psychological science: never before has man been so directly or so deeply confronted
with his own particular mystery.

Sexuality and Religious Uneasiness

With regard to its sexuality as a life experience, the
human race has always found itself in a situation of uneasiness, if not even of fear. And this reaction is always

bound up with religious uneasiness in general, whether that be explicitly recognized or not.

Many examples of this may be drawn from different kinds of civilization. We shall consider but two human outlooks, however, both of which are meaningful from this point of view.

The first instance is the strange custom of ritual circumcision. From the hygienic and surgical point of view, circumcision is an operation whose purpose is to facilitate the physiological changes in the sexual organ and to help keep clean that part of the body especially susceptible to different types of infection.

It seems quite clear, however, that the ancient East did not regard circumcision in this light, nor, for that matter, do present-day Orthodox Jews. In their eyes, circumcision is a purely ritual and not a medical action, that is to say, there is question of an outlook of life dependent on an Other, supposed or real, multiple or unique—an "other-than-the-human-world," a "Superior Being."

On the symbolic and psychological level, two aspects of circumcision stand out in apparent contradiction. On the one hand, what takes place is a "cutting," a "falling-away of something," with reference to the uniquely specifying object—the phallus. On the other hand, circumcision makes the object appear to be unmistakably a phallus; the "sheathed," specifically masculine, is freed from the "sheath," specifically feminine. The sexual differentiation is thereby established. In broad daylight, so to speak, the phallus affirms itself as such, freed from restraint and from what disguises it. Sexuality, as such, is clearly revealed, and its relations with individual death is not to be forgotten.

A peculiarly Freudian interpretation has its foundation in one aspect of the "castration anguish" discovered by analysis at a particular point in the child's evolution. Granted, this interpretation has merely hypothetical value, still there is foundation in the following analogy with individual emotional evolution.

The "primitive human herd" lived under the absolute and undisputed authority of the leader who had forcibly imposed himself upon them. To make sure of his place, the leader was accustomed to emasculate his sons. But the time came when the sons, evidently protected by the women, escaped this castration. Their position then became one of rivalry. The sons could now come into control of the same power as their father and take his place in a life-or-death showdown. The "murder of the father" and the fear of murder itself, as well as the fear of being killed by the father who would not tolerate any rivalry—these new themes of civilization brought in tensions that had to be settled. In this way was introduced the custom of a "symbolic" castration offered to the father to quiet his anger. Should it be conceded that the first religious refinements are a projection of the primitive fear of the father, then ritual circumcision assumes this meaning.

However, this hypothesis accounts for only one side of this very complex problem: the "castration" aspect. It does not take into account the "disengagement-from-the-object" aspect. And, from the point of view of the primitive psychological working out of the body's image, this second aspect is at least of equal importance.

With the coming of Judaic revelation, everything takes on new meaning and direction. According to the first hypothesis, circumcision, characterized by the need of casting out a primitive fear, on God's order now becomes the explicit sign of a covenant with this Other-than-the-world who, as opposed to all other gods, speaks, questions, and demands. This reversal has its importance. The motive for undergoing this rite is no longer fear, but a promise of fidelity. Circumcision becomes the primordial sign of belonging to the "People of Yahweh" who stresses his unapproachability even as He affirms his presence, who "makes being," who is the Creator of the world and of life. It should be carefully noted that this idea of a unique principle at the origin of everything is absolutely new in human religious thought at this time in history. Only in the later developments of Greek thought will this idea be found, and that because of the Greek penchant for philosophical abstraction. Yahweh is, therefore, the ultimate, personal fruitfulness: his word causes existence; he raises up life and power. In this absolutely new context, circumcision (which reveals and sets free the very mysterious object which is the seat of power and fecundity) is seen as a real furtherance of sexuality, and on God's order. Its written formula is founded in the Genesis perspective of "increase and multiply." The idea of fruitfulness in the Covenant with Yahweh is one of the important themes of Hebraic thought. This "cult of fruitfulness" is by no means similar to the fertility cult of the "Linga," for example, evidence of whose activities are to be seen in the various temples of Angkor. The object of adoration is not symbolic Sex; it is a God standing completely above and beyond sexuality. Opportunities to obey his order of existence are afforded in human sexuality.

Yet, despite all that, the anguish has not been settled. This is but a stage. Bit by bit, Judaic revelation, particularly along the prophetic line, was leading men to a new discovery: the meaning of death. When the Christian religion exploded on the world, especially under the leadership of Paul (who, until the time of Damascus, was a fanatical "circumcised"), the sign of belonging assumed a more developed level of meaning, that of baptism. No longer was the Christian religion predominantly one of fertility (the relative character of fecundity had now been deeply grasped); it was now a religion of death, of salvation, of fulfillment, and of an approach to that transcendent life of the Other-who-spoke, even to the point of his personal entry into human history.

With no intention of forcing the meaning of things, it seems that the forward movement of the Judaeo-

Christian line may be expressed in this way: the Other-who-speaks, first of all, frees humanity in its sexual condition from the prison of primitive anguish by changing the meaning of ritual circumcision; then he came in person to curb the excesses of the sexual (in the strict sense) and to resolve its ambivalence beyond limited human possibilities. We shall, of course, develop these observations more fully later on.

The other fear perspective connected with sexuality is, reducibly, what we call "taboo," and it has many different manifestations.

First of all, there is the conspiracy of silence: "We simply do not talk about that." Sexuality is precisely a taboo-subject: the very mention of the topic is certain to unleash occult forces that have a sort of autonomy productive of evil and of catastrophic doom. Proof of this is found in puritanical forms of education. Life must go on, preferably sealed off from this area of sexuality, the very province in which man is so vibrant and so uniquely sensitive and which evidences the fact of his separation. Taboos are blind to the facts of life: through sexuality a baby abandons life within his mother's body to become separated and to discover himself; through sexuality one adult becomes fully alive with desire of a definite relationship with another; through sexuality the dialectic of anguish, as we now use the term, reaches a pinnacle. The very effort to isolate sexual reality, whose manifestations are a matter of everyday experience, betrays a rudimentary psychic reaction. To deny sexual reality or to try to suppress it and remove it from the human reality is, in a word, genuine "castration by fear." The only tolerable image of the other (and, by projection, an image of self) is a desexualized image, that is to say, one which isolates that unique region where a "lack," the "fear of a lack," or the "lack of a lack" is indicated. Basically, the behavior-forms of extreme modesty are grouped along this line, and they are the result of sullen submission or of mocking irony. This archaic fear of the sexual is inaugurated by the mere idea that a desire can be desired if it may be realized in expression. For example, its pre-logical character is shown in the different forms of indignation raised against the increasing scantiness of bathing suits—and this, although experience offers abundant proof that quasi-nudity in public tends rather to do away with desire (doubtlessly, through psychological mechanisms which themselves are quite complex).

Another aspect of taboo is seen in a certain uneasy overevaluation of sexual behavior with regard to its moral qualification. For example, in certain types of spirituality, control of the sex life, traditionally called chastity (which has a very positive meaning), is known as the "holy virtue." Such overevaluation tends to place the other virtues in the position of being less holy or less fundamental. Truth is clearly distorted in such a case in light of the most explicit teaching of Christ and His

Church: *the* virtue, whose sovereignty is absolute and which gives form to all other virtues, is charity, or love— love, obviously, that transcends sexual love. St. Thomas Aquinas, for example, regards chastity as but a part of the virtue of temperance, whose true value consists purely in its relation to charity. And spiritual directors are actually deploring this taboo when they complain of the total ignorance about sex among aspirants to religious life. Ignorance, they say, is not purity.

This overevaluation of everything connected with genital sexuality means, at the same time, that sexual sins are regarded as more appalling than even deliberate sins against justice. A married man will be petrified by fear after practicing interrupted intercourse; yet, that same man will think nothing at all about the sins of pride in his life. There is no proper reflection or evaluation in the too easy, almost instinctive, regarding of sexual sins as the worst of all possible offenses. This is nothing but a case of taboo: everything connected with genital sexuality causes fear and strange awe. Confirmation of this is too readily found in what are literally "pan-sexualist" statements of traditional moral theology. Not so long ago, for example, there were some moralists who held that the marital sexual act is a "permitted sin."

This "fear" can take on another form. There are moralists (and it must be stressed that it makes no difference whether they are Catholic or not) who admit the possibility of distinguishing between the moral evaluation of sexual behavior in the abstract and properly assessing the moral activity of a given subject in this or that concrete life-situation. This classical distinction calls for rather delicate handling (and casuists at times seem to use it for introducing moral relativism into some fields of morality). To be of any use, however, it must be well understood. When efforts are made to state the distinction or to apply it accurately to sexual behavior, a storm of protest is raised among certain individuals: "Don't talk about that too much. It could be dangerous!" Yet, these same people are unable to specify the danger feared; they are unable to pinpoint the reason why they are afraid that "a loosening of morals will result" regarding sex. And, yet, in an area outside sexuality, sins against social injustice leave such people emotionally undisturbed.

Finally, in literature or in certain parts of the movie industry, an opposite aspect of the taboo may be detected in an overevaluation of erotism as such. At first, this situation seems to be anything but a manifestation of fear, and to link it up with taboo may certainly appear paradoxical. But it, too, is dependent upon that very primitive and very ambivalent fascination with the sexual mystery.

The tendency is to explain this reaction of taboo by the rise and intensification of primitive social prohibitions. The fear of castration by the father, the fear of the son's murder of his father as well as other such fears doubtlessly have something to do with taboo. Yet, withal, they do not seem to go to the heart of the matter sufficiently, and they still account for only a superficial aspect of the phenomenon.

The origin of these instinctive fears (which, as taboo shows, continue to exist in a vague form) must be sought in two constitutive aspects of sexuality itself in the form in which we have already presented them.

The first is the fundamental dialectic of anguish. Sexuality occasions the separation, the cause of separate existence; sexuality also brings about the uncontrollable ambivalence involved in the relation to the other.

Next follows the strange fact that sexuality is just as much bound up with death as with life. A sexed being transmits life without self-disappearance, but, as we noted earlier, it is already on the way to its own death. On the level of his general sexuality, and not merely in its exercise, man retreats from the world about him, a fact which establishes him as a self-conscious being, therefore a being different from the animal. Is it paradoxical to say that man, by this very self-consciousness, is brought face-to-face with his personal mortal condition? Not actually in the sense of a conscious and reflex confrontation, although this could also happen, of course, in which case man would later know how to keep death at a distance. However, we are referring here to a confrontation that is literally indefinable because it occupies a place "before everything else," and which, only much later, man will more fully understand and be able to articulate. We may call this the initial, or in-augural, or "constitutive" confrontation.

An in-depth analysis of desire is needed at this point in the general meaning of desire as well as in its sexual denotation. Just what is desire? With what profound lack is it associated? Why is it always so illusory that, al-though satisfied in the form that it takes, it is always springing up again? And why, right up to the moment of death, is man always and endlessly subject to desire of some sort or other? And is not desire, as such, always "an accessory" of "what is lacking" and capable of being viewed in this light only in the presence of death?

Furthermore, what precisely is sexual desire in the strict sense, that desire experienced in an explicit rela-tionship to another person on the phantasmal, imagi-nary, or symbolic level? Full analysis of this query would require an extended treatise all its own.

In any case, our everyday language does have its own way of expressing this mystery of sexuality. The expres-sion "little death" is often used to express orgasm. The strong desire, the emotional intensity involved in orgasm, the "slumping" of the phallus—that is, detumescence which accompanies orgasm and sperm emission and which, biologically, is not a universal or necessary phe-nomenon—all so many lived realities that unavoidably suggest a close relationship between desire, "castration," and death. Man asks woman to participate in an extra-ordinary and complex experience "just for the two of

them" (with a "third"—the child—possible, whether wanted, feared, or prevented), and the experience has just as much to do with death as with life.

But why is death so unbearable to us? For example, there are people who cannot stand the notion of killing a wild deer or the sight of a bleeding chicken, yet these are the very ones who will madly rush off to a public execution. As these people explain it, they have no fear of a death "which leads to nothing."

The real origin of taboo in all its manifestations must certainly be sought on the level of these obscure fears and of these poorly worked out sublimations of primordial anguish, in the meaning we have assigned to anguish.

Mysterious sexuality: it is the existential crossroads of consciousness of self in relation to the other, of being and of time, of life and of death.

that minimal degree necessary for further normal development—that is to say, without pathological manifestations in the strict sense. Relations with the surrounding world take on a definite educative note inasmuch as, in the fashion of a verbal dialogue, true self-understanding begins.

Such, in brief outline, is the so-called "hidden" period which begins about seven years of age and for which there is no threshold that can be exactly pinpointed. This "hidden" period corresponds, for all practical purposes, with what we regard as the age of reason.

Adolescence at Puberty

At this stage, the gradual growing of the psychosomatic personality comes to a head with a rather abrupt change of rhythm. When a pan of water is being heated, what takes place is a gradual thing, a growing in intensity. Suddenly the water starts to boil. Quarrel with the example, if you will, but it will serve to illustrate the explosive character of adolescence.

Adolescence begins at puberty, and there is no need here to detail its manifestations. During this period the secondary sexual characteristics quickly assert themselves, and the individual now has the bodily form which will remain unchanged throughout his life, except for some non-essential variations. Physically, the sexual organs attain their functional maturity, as shown in the case of the girl by her menstruation and, in the case of the boy, by emission of the sperm.

Much more important, and what should be underscored, is the psycho-affective aspect of this fairly rude explosion.

The relation of the subject to the other inaugurates a meaningful change. His whole inclination is to abandon a position of dependency, perfectly satisfactory up to this time, in favor of a spirit of freedom from control, and this change in inclination is reflected in an upheaval in conduct. Conflict inevitably arises, and it makes its first appearance with those around him. Up to that time, the parents' attitude was accepted as perfectly natural; now the subject begins seriously to question it. The adolescent is inclined to live on his own, and he has no further intention to submit to guidance or protection. We have no intention of being flattering when we speak about youth's manifesto of independence, about youth in revolt, about youth unchecked, about youth's rebellion against law and order. Yet, we should try to understand that these youthful reactions are more emotional than sensible and that they do not really indicate a youth's complete rejection of efforts to have him mingle socially. Once we know these adolescent reactions for what they fundamentally are, we shall cease to look upon them as revolt. Youth is not brushing aside the world of adults; it is merely asking for a form of recognition it never had until this stage of development. Youth wants to display its own initiative; it never sufficiently stressed. The very settling of the identification-conflict opens up a satisfying approach to the psychological possibility of social life. By transferring from the *dual* relationship (to the parent of the opposite sex) to the *triangular* relationship, the child has opened its arms to his or her future marriage partner, to his or her future children, to all possible relations with other men and women, and it does so in the basic emotional security that makes such relations possible. In passing, let it be said that it is really remarkable, from the psychological viewpoint, that it is absolutely necessary to pass from a "relation of two" to a "relation of three" in order that the whole of existence, self-realization and love may be truly possible. This "triangular moment" is one of the primordial elements of modern psychology. Every "hardened Oedipus," independently of formally sexual symptoms, is a perennial source of difficulty with regard to social integration. In a word, it is a question here of spelling out the primitive dialectic ("return-to-the-womb anguish") of which we spoke before.

The Latent Period

Once the child has resolved the Oedipus crisis by way of wholesome identification with the parent of the same sex, it finds itself in a kind of provisional period of satisfaction and emotional security. It has been successful in finding a suitable and deeply satisfying place in the real world around it. This sense of security, however, cannot guarantee the reoccurrence of conflicts and crises. But the nature of these onslaughts is apparent to the child, and they prove precisely this, that the identification which settled the Oedipus crisis, as it were, is a *distinguishing* identification, or better, a *personalizing* identification. An eight-year-old child who was so completely a "carbon copy" as never to offer opposition would, from the point of view of psychic health, have all the ingredients of a rather alarming future.

What is important, moreover, is that this first effervescence of spirits during the first six or seven years could culminate in the subject's discovery of its own sexuality. For the moment, this awareness of identity assures the child of a well-balanced existence in its relations to the world about it. The child has a good grasp of itself and has a solid enough foundation not to be brushed off as a questionable case at the level of anguish (as we have defined anguish) by even the conflicting circumstances of its life, and to the degree that its life is somewhat normal.

In its relation to itself, therefore, the child has acquired a form of basic emotional soundness which allows for free development of what we refer to as the superior faculties—the autonomous intellect and will. The child's need to know, to understand and to assume proper responsibilities shows that, on the level of awareness and disclosure, a sublimation has been reached, at least in

II

SOME PHYSIOLOGICAL ASPECTS OF MODERN ANTHROPOLOGY

example: Can the child leave the world of imaginings (primitive, unconscious images of himself and of the other) and be itself rather than the partial, narcissistic object of its father and mother. To answer this, however, would involve us in considerations which would probably divert us from the general course of our investigation.

The "Oedipus" Crisis

What we have observed here regarding the child's development necessarily implies a relationship with real parents. It is precisely from this relationship that there arises, in outline form, a crisis which is going to mark the end of the first years of personality development and which is known, symbolically, as the "Oedipus" crisis.

The small boy enters into a real relationship of rivalry and defiance with the father over the matter of preferential treatment by the mother. The little boy's imagining the father's departure from the scene and "pairing with the mother," coupled with his reverting to such earlier habits as bed-wetting and baby talk, marks this stage of conflict. Actually, the "desire to overcome the father" evokes the fear of "castration" or of death. The crisis can be settled only by the acceptance of symbolic castration: the young boy must completely stop wanting to be "the phallus of the mother," must stop regarding the father as "the phallus *par excellence*." The personality is, so to speak, cut away from the phallic object which discovers its symbolic place in the representation of the ego.

In the case of the young girl, relationship with the father predominates: he is the phallus which she does not possess, but which the mother does, in a certain sense, possess by her marriage. Rivalry springs up. The young girl will integrate her own lack of a phallus in a "symbolic castration" of the father: now the object, as such, loses its primitive importance in order to make way for the subject. From that point on, the young girl is prepared to see not the *phallus*, but him who has the phallus. At that point, instinctive sexual orientation has been acquired.

The child brings this struggle to an end by the process of identification. Whereas, earlier, the child wanted to subjugate the parent of its own sex, now the same child tends to take that parent as a "successful prototype" of what it must itself become. In the course of playing the mature "lady of the house," the little girl parades about the apartment with her mother's hat and purse, while the little boy imitates the language and actions of his father. This is by no means simply a slavish copying; rather, I daresay, this stage of taking inspiration from the parent of the same sex marks the beginning of *developing* its own sexed personality in the normal child.

One very important aspect of the Oedipus crisis is

sphincter muscles. In highlighting the theme of this stage of development, it is no exaggeration to say that the child experiences a distinct and important satisfaction in its performance: it has given form to something which comes out of it—and it did so by itself. In reality, it is the child's first creation; furthermore, it is a response made to a request in a love-relation so essential to the child. An aspect of loss, of "cutting," of the "falling-away of something" is also involved here. Perhaps we can better understand the significance of this loss by equating it with the artist who, on the emotional level, has "given his all." Once again, the proportionate play of pleasure and fear places the child in a position to confront and to overcome this fear of "losing itself" and to make progress along the road of evolving sublimation.

The Genital Stage

Genital sexuality, properly so called, is included, but imperceptibly, in emotional life. Anatomically and physiologically, both the anal and genital zones are very close to one another and have great solidarity in the matter of sensitivity. The next stage for the child—the genital stage—consists in its discovery of the sensitivity and meaning of its genital sexuality. One is tempted to remark here, "Everything new, everything lovely," because the revelation of genital sexuality is about to occupy front and center stage. It is, at one and the same time, a terminal and a point of departure, because from now on the child will achieve a consciousness of itself precisely from its sexuality.

The child's instinctive attention is directed to the genital area. From examination of the parts, the child will experience sensations wholly new to it. People still consider this innocent form of exploration as the bad habit of a naughty child, but certainly no question of moral behavior is involved here. Granted the importance of this emotional discovery and its inherent intensity, consider now the harm adults may do by blaming the child: development may be blocked; the child may be brought to face almost insurmountable conflicts which, in turn, may lead to seriously neurotic difficulties in the future.

At this stage, the presence or absence of the phallic object assumes first place in the affective life of the child. For the small boy, the phallic object becomes the symbol of himself, his personal distinction. Absence of the phallic object, in the case of the little girl, becomes a primordial "question." To indicate only the essential line of development, let it be said that, during this stage, the child is going to "liquidate" the castration fear, properly so called, that is, the fear of losing or of having lost the phallic object. Of course, there are many other considerations in this genital stage, viewed in the light of the earlier development of the child's relation to the phallic object in general. There is this question, for

It is important, regarding the "ego," to realize that it is not a kind of "super-added reality." The "it," the "super-ego," and the "ego" are neither things nor entities. They are ways of expressing what really takes place in the normal development of the child. At the start of a given age (especially at the beginning of the so-called age of reason), the problem has to do with the child's becoming more and more capable, by itself, of questioning the "counter-drives" of his super-ego. Finally, it would be ideal to have everything explained, neatly outlined, free of primitive fears and refined into such clear, moral independence as would, generally speaking, be wholly directed toward the "relation to the other." This, in the language of Christianity, is exactly what Christ wanted as the starting place of every action. This ideal, however, is never reached. The standard practice is, in fact, to return to a childish "pre-moral" attitude. In the case of some moralists, this occasionally reaches the point of deadening or seriously distorting true spiritual progress.

Evolution

The child's sex, as well as its relation to real persons, is a basic condition for the rearing of its own personality. This occurs gradually and ceaselessly. The child struggles to make its sexual personality whole on every level—

organic, sensory, emotional, imaginary, and symbolic. In the discernible development, so-called "stages" may be distinguished. A better expression should be found because "stages" connotes a short rest-stop, a place where things come to a halt. All that can be said is that the one looking on becomes aware, every so often, that "something new is taking place," the more or less clear traces of which are brought to light in and through the analytic exploration of adult life.

Oral Stage

In the beginning, eating controls the whole emotional life. This is the "oral" stage. Desire in its widest meaning, enjoyment and displeasure occur essentially on this level which can be said to contain virtually all the levels to be revealed in due course. The oral relation is already sexual and involves the forecast of further disclosures. By comparison, the whole plant can be said to be present, virtually and dynamically, in the grain of living wheat cast into the ground.

The Anal Stage

The little child succeeds in its first real and unaided experiment when, on instruction, it is able to control its

In his desire to poke fun at the physicians of his day Molière put the two Diafoirus on stage and had them take a strong position against the theory of blood circulation. To understand the point, it should be recalled that, although the discovery of this essential physiological function was scarcely fifty years old, it had been solidly confirmed by the British physician Harvey. In other words, the Diafoirus were just as silly as any physician today who would mock the discovery of X-rays.

Now this reference should make us aware that the circulation of the blood was unknown until the early seventeenth century. Until that time, anatomical studies were conducted according to scientific methods in vogue at the end of the Middle Ages. For one thing, dissection of cadavers had to be made legally possible instead of remaining a practice kept secret because of religious interdicts. Physiological knowledge was at its first prattling stage, and it was only with Claude Bernard that physiology became organized as a distinct science. Without the least exaggeration, we may state that man never really even began to *know* about his various bodily functions until the beginning of this twentieth century. It is almost impossible to imagine the chasm between how men of the seventeenth and twentieth centuries viewed themselves.

The modern middle-class man does not breathe, eat, or move about in the same way as did his ancestor of several hundred years ago. Today, man knows about the proper working condition of his lungs and how to take care of his digestion in order to avoid stomach discomfort. He knows so much that sometimes it makes the work of the physician difficult; the patient claims to know almost as much as his doctor.

Consider also the role which photography was to play. Until its invention, the vast majority of men had only a reverse view of themselves in a mirror. Modern man has gotten a new look at himself: the view which others have of him, and he has had this view from his early childhood. Granted the importance of the first acquirings of one's identity, it is not a casual matter that the child

to be preserved in its entirety for fecundity under pain
of serious sin—harks back to the ages of symbolic or
mythical knowledge. It no longer has validity in the face
of physiological knowledge which portrays the sperm
as an intermittent and special organic secretion, teeming
with male cells at n/2 chromosomes, of which the quasi-
totality is fated for destruction pure and simple. It is
amazing to realize that, out of the few liters of sperm
which the average man can produce between the time
of puberty and death—literally incalculable billions of
spermatozoa—only eight, at most, will have played a
part in the event, let us say, that he has four children.

Let this fact of science, then, free moral concepts from
crass material considerations. The "sacred anguish" on
losing the seed no longer has meaning in the eyes of modern science. The search for moral values must be made on
a higher plane, the plane of intersubjective relations
and of the meaning of sexuality. Unquestionably, there
is need of further reflection here.

With regard to the production of these seminal cells,
another observation comes to mind. Whether it be the
case of the ovule or the spermatozoa, these cells are the
result of a very particular and unique process in physiology: they comprise only half of the chromosomes that
give the breed definite form. In order to be fecundated
or to produce fecundation—that is, in order to be specifically sexual, these cells must lose something, nothing
less than half of their nuclear potential. Here again, on

the organic level itself, we discover this strange necessity of the *separation*, of *loss*, which alone can effect the genital cellular reaction and the formation of the egg, that is, of an individual that is new, distinct, although not yet "separated."

Male Physiology

Many people compare the activity of the male sexual organism to the other physiological processes by which waste matter is evacuated from the body, such as processes of micturition or defecation. These people speak as though there were somewhere a continuing storing up of sperm ("informed" minds speak of seminal vesicles) which insistently call for release when the container is full to the brim. This phenomenon, they say, carries sexual desire in its wake.

If this were really the case, every man with a normal constitution would experience a sexual desire—and the insistent organic necessity of satisfying it—according to a rhythm just about as regular and inevitable as kidney or bowel action. And right here the Kinsey Report makes some very interesting points. Nothing varies so much as the rhythm of the physiological function of masculine sexuality. Consider two extremes: the thirty-five-year-old celibate who produces only two or three nocturnal ejaculations in a year; the man who engages in daily intercourse, yet produces five or six ejaculations yearly.

comes the principal object of this encounter. What happens here may be described as the baby's efforts "to fit in with what the mother expects of it" in order not to lose the maternal love which is just as important as is milk to the baby's life. The very first traces of *purposeful* behavior occur in the baby in accordance with the mother's image of the baby, an image to which the baby tries to conform. This very first sketch of a "self-image," on the most obscure level, is necessarily a succession, by turns, of "do" and "don't." In this way, the "premoral organism," known as the *super-ego,* begins to develop in the baby.

The baby must be understood as naturally in need of love, of being in a relation where it is known to be personally valuable in the eyes of the other. And this need exists from the very moment of its birth, if not before. Experiments clearly show that this kind of relation is absolutely necessary for the nursing baby in order that it may assimilate its food. Without such relation (experienced with the mother or her substitute), the baby's bodily health is jeopardized; and even its very life is threatened. This is the specifically human element. And the love which the baby receives allows it to evolve in the sense of that sublimation of which we spoke in connection with anguish.

The child's reactions are inextricably bound to this love, and such love must not be taken away. Every prohibition by the mother is regarded as a threat to this needed love. Instinctively the child will deny itself what is forbidden.

Next, even in the baby's unclear vision the mother is seen as bound to the father. Gradually the father assumes importance. The father becomes the "fixed reference-point," whose word is law, a forbidding figure as well as protective. Once these prohibitions, increasing in number and kind, become part of the small child, they constitute the basic strata of what will later be the personal moral life, properly so called. And it is altogether too easy for irrational notions, false values, and primordial fears to be passed on to the child; in other words, everything that is in the unconscious of the parents, that has remained unclarified, not thought through. Besides, there is nothing astonishing in the fact that such fears, prejudices, and abnormal values should, generally speaking, be more intense regarding sexual matters than for any other areas of existence.

Suppose a blindfolded person were shut up in a dark room and told to find his way out. At first, of course, he would grope for an exit. After he had bumped into a table, a chair, a wall, or other obstacles, he would gradually become oriented. From this point on, he would be able to think more clearly, then find the door. Now, probably some psychoanalysts will disagree with this allegorical way of explaining the developing of the "ego." Granted, it is arguable. At the same time, it will give the lay reader some clue to the essentials.

in which the *other* (whoever he may be) is himself more and more regarded as an equal and a distinct subject. Self-awareness, "being one's self alone," this freedom which is experienced in one's life and which is rooted in one's makeup—pathology makes this very clear—is brought into the open only in the relation that is lived. And this relation, so imprecise at the start, never arrives at complete being and is never fully freed from the determining factors which are its foundation in being and from which it takes origin. So that Corneille's famous line to the effect that each of us is master of himself and of the universe is rather silly for the pride it expresses; and it becomes downright ridiculous in the light of modern psychology.

Were I a sculptor, I should symbolically represent freedom by the statue of a human bust springing forth from the original clay, arms stretched heavenward. And this bust would, of necessity, be sexed.

The Beginnings

The main, basic Freudian concepts are now fairly widely known. There is always the risk that they may become hardened into a rigid and abstract system and that their essential nature, dynamism and symbolism may be forgotten. It cannot be repeated too often that, much more so than any other scientific language, the language of modern psychology both voices and betrays, at one and the same time, the living reality which it seeks to make known.

There can be no question here of becoming involved in the interminable research-work peculiar to this field. We deliberately intend to limit ourselves to recalling, in an orderly way, certain matters essential for understanding sexual evolution or, more exactly, for understanding the development of what can only be a sexed personality.

The newly-born baby's fundamental, existential dynamisms are strong, but not yet adapted to external objects. If "instincts" will do as a description of them, the whole of this instinctive power of living is notable for its lack of clarity and organization. This is called the "it" for the very reason that this instinctive power, which is both primordial and "anonymous," defies accurate description.

The baby is immediately ushered into its adaptation. It must, equally immediately, behave in other than a purely instinctive way and build up the first lines of its behavior patterns. Its blind, instinctive[1] drives are called into play "by chance," and these drives are immediately opposed by surroundings. The mother be-

---

[1] This expression is subject of regular dispute. "Drive" is too easily confused with what, in an adult, is the deep, dynamic force of certain forms of behavior.

and which, at the beginning, exists only virtually, is essentially dynamic, evolving, and infinitely outgoing.

We mentioned earlier that man's instinct is faulty as a guide to what he must do to survive in life. It follows, then, that man must assure his living in an altogether different way.

Because he is able to see himself "from in front" as others see him, man will gradually work out his own way of doing things. The very first signs of this are rather faint, but, radically, they are already different from a simple reflex. Position in life, outlook, actions—all these seem pretty much the same at first glance: all babies nurse in the same way; they begin to stand up and walk at about the same age. However, beneath this apparent identity of pattern it is not hard to see that there is already a struggle for expression which is different every time. Each small child takes its place in the world, according to a general plan, but each child executes that plan in its own way. The moment the child begins to scrutinize something, there begins what must be called the mystery of personal questioning. This explains the difficulties in education: a dog is trained because it does not think; a child, however, is capable of its own thought, even though the thought may be contrary to what is being taught.

The analysis of the first stages and what remains of them in the adult's ability to adapt himself to the world about him (in particular, the child's "mirror period") give a fairly clear idea of the long-lasting efforts involved in finding self-identity, efforts which take up the first years of each one's personal history. Each of us, in some way, is formed by these efforts which are each time new, personal, and unique. Consider, for one thing, this difference between the human and the animal: the female dog gives birth to a litter of puppies; the baby normally is born in one particular moment in the personal history of its parents, a moment always different from those when his brothers and sisters were born.

By seizing upon his self-identity in his relation to the world, the baby will be able gradually to assume for himself his own adaptation to reality; instinct alone is not enough for this. Only at the end of a certain time does this reflex knowledge become conscious knowledge; eventually, however, a startling phenomenon occurs on the day when the child no longer speaks of himself as of another person, but says "I." Note that he says it, and necessarily so, to someone or in dependence on someone. As Lacan says, the child never speaks alone. Even when he is taken by surprise in a monologue, he is actually speaking as would an actor to someone off stage, that is, dependently on another "interior" person.

Freedom may, perhaps, be described in this way: that advance of self-knowledge in the dialogue with the other (no matter who he may be) which allows each *subject,* in accord with his independent responsibility, to take an active part in a more and more developed dialogue

The Human History of Sexuality

Beyond Instinct

Man stands before the world in unique originality in virtue of his own existential adaptation to that world. His originality includes both a peculiar weakness and a striking greatness. In all of nature, man alone is conscious of nature. This fact is as well known as Pascal's celebrated phrase, "the thinking reed." Because man alone is conscious of nature, he is placed in a certain solitude, so that, in one sense, every man is a summary and an expression of his solitary situation. It is not at all too paradoxical to remark that all thought, all knowledge and all of philosophy is the result of an immense effort to communicate these solitudes, each of which is aware of itself.

True, it was not necessary to have waited for Freud in the nineteenth century so to describe the human state of affairs. At the same time, it was Freud's discoveries which, for the first time in human history, allows entry into that zone of the human condition which is concrete and visible and which yet eludes the reflection of reason for the very good reason that its precedes rational reflection. Looking into the psychic world of the young child from the very outset of its existence has been made possible, as has the knowledge of the conditioning of each personality, by the beginnings of adaptation.

Rational reflection cannot help but be profoundly changed by this; nor, as I see it, has the full extent of the change been grasped. The nature of this change can be stated, for the moment, by setting up an opposition to certain accepted definitions of man. The old Aristotelian definition, "Man is a rational animal," can hardly be considered satisfactory; it is entirely too abstract and oversimplified. How, then, may man be defined in the light of this new knowledge? At this point, we shall venture only this definition: "Every human being, specifically different from the animal, is a living being which gives light to itself and which, while continuing to establish its vital relations, strives with all its being to make its love fully real, yet never reaching that goal." Love in this definition is by no means limited to its sexual dimensions. This "light to itself," which specifies man

The functioning of masculine sexuality (something continually misunderstood) is quite clearly no more a necessary organic rhythmic process for the male human than it is for any male animal. Now, if any comparison is to be made with the functioning of male sexuality, the salivary glands should be thought of rather than the bladder or the intestines. Nevertheless, it must be remembered that the digestive function, toward which the salivary glands are directed, is required for the life of the organism, something which is not true of the sexual function, as the Kinsey Report has well pointed out.

The salivary glands always work at a slow pace. However, when they are aroused, either by the senses or the imagination, they then cause abundant salivation for Pavlov's dog equally as for the gourmand.

Man's genital apparatus comprises a system of glands, a system of deferent ducts, an erectile organ, and a special ejaculatory duct. The entire organism is fully equipped with nerves and is lubricated.

The glands are, essentially, the two testicles, the two seminal vesicles (in no sense reservoirs), the prostate, and some other glands of no particular importance. At the level of the prostate are joined, in a common exit, the two symmetrical deferent ducts which, on each side, correspond to the testicle and to the seminal vesicle. This outlet is located at the posterier part of the prostate in the upper part of the urethral canal which it surrounds, at the exit of the bladder, like a ring whose stone-setting would be at the back. At the beginning of its passageway the urethral (urinary) canal comprises a zone called the intra-prostatic bulb which makes possible future genital functions. Above and below the prostate, two circular muscles (sphincters) are able to close the ureter very tightly. The one above is voluntary, the one below is a muscle which functions in a reflex manner. In this way, the limits are set up for a virtual "reservoir," the intra-prostatic bulb, which is capable eventually of being closed off by the two sphincters and of being approached only by the liquid carried in the genital ducts.

In its ordinary calm state (and experience shows that, unlike other organic functions, this can continue for months), the entire glandular system functions "in low gear." The testicles produce only a few spermatozoa; the seminal vesicles and the prostate produce only a small amount of their respective liquids. At the moment of micturition, everything is emptied out through the urethral canal, a safeguard against drying up, just as saliva is for the buccal mucous.

However, given stimulation—whether it comes from the mind, the senses or the imagination and regardless of whether the man be aware of it or not, awake or asleep —an intense physiological activity starts up. A quick flow of blood is produced. Under pressure, the erectile organ swells with blood; the arteries which terminate there are dilated, and the veins leading out from there are contracted. The various glands increase their functional activity. The two sphincters close up, micturition becomes impossible, and the "genital reservoir" of the urethral bulb is set up. Obviously, if the excitation ceases, this comes to a stop, either spontaneously or in one or other voluntary way.

Should the stimulation continue and increase in intensity, then, of course, the whole process moves toward completion. Tension in the erectile organ increases from the rhythmical rubbing (in intercourse, or manually, or in some other similar way). In the final moments, the prostatic fluid, that of the vesicles, and spermatozoa are all produced in greater quantity, are mixed and collected in the introprostatic bulb; the rapid filling of the intraprostatic bulb then sets off the ejaculatory mechanism. The accompanying sensation is generally intense, although it varies greatly according to the psychological conditions in which it is experienced. The ejaculation is followed almost at once by the erectile organ's going limp (which takes more time in animals) and by the return to a normal blood circulation.

Sexual desire and its concomitant tension are certainly not caused by the formation or accumulation of sperm. The truth is the exact opposite. Desire and sexual activity in man are essentially a process of psychic origin.

Female Physiology

In the case of the woman, everything physiologically associated with sexuality, occurs in a different way. The periods which affect her genital life are implanted in her very physiology. The difference between the animal and the human makeup is most readily apparent from a knowledge of female physiology.

The female genital apparatus comprises particular glands, the organ of gestation, the uterus, and the way of access and expulsion (the vagina and vulva), completely separated from the neighboring urinary tract.

The woman's specific glands—the ovaries—contain, as it were, the whole duration of the woman's genital life (from puberty to the menopause), virtually implanted in their covering layer.

Beginning with puberty and through a cycle which is theoretically regular, this superficial layer produces, at a point on its surface, an isolated genital cell—the ovule —which is also evaluated at n/2 chromosomes. When the follicle which contains the ovule becomes mature, it bursts, and then the ovule falls into the tubes leading to the uterus.

As this process of maturing proceeds, a very complex operation takes place in the genital tract. Two principal hormones play their part in a proportionately varying activity: the hormone secreted by the follicle and that secreted by the scar tissue which replaces it. This scar tissue is called the lutein, or the yellow body. At the beginning, the first hormone is clearly more abundant, then starts to decrease; the second hormone, on the contrary, comes on the scene and increases during the course of the cycle; then, in turn, it also begins to de-not only attributes the acquiring of this identity to the inverted mirror-image which he recognizes as his own, but also bases this acquisition on the direct photographic image of himself, in which case he looks upon himself as though he were somebody other than himself. Photography certainly has played a real part in man's efforts to acquire a consciousness of his self.

All the scientific findings on the physiology of sexuality are registered in this whole context. "Basic anthropology" today (by that I mean the representation which modern man makes of himself) has no common denominator with the knowledge at the disposal of man a century and a half ago. The high-school graduate today has an infinitely wider knowledge of the world and of himself than the greatest intellectuals of the eighteenth century.

Yet, knowledge of and the language to express the human concern of sexuality—aside, of course, from moral teachings—remains in a state corresponding to sixteenth-century anthropology. This time-lag is a disgrace and accounts for all the blind alleys and the obscurantism regarding true values. And birth-control is a case in point.

If efforts to advance progress in both ideas and language are desirable, then some aspects of scientific findings on the level of physiology must be made to stand out in bold relief. Any attempt to improve a dismal situation involves highlighting scientific findings, particularly those of physiology. That will be our next concern.

Superabundance

This is an outstanding fact: to an incredible degree, male seed components outnumber female ovules; in other words, for each ovule produced by the woman during intercourse, the man provides, in one teaspoon of sperm, billions of spermatozoa. Of these, usually only one or two will reach the ovule and fertilize it. All the others are lost. Biological nature involves conspicuous waste. This well-known truth is broadcast by popular science, illustrations, documentary films, and the like.

Physiologically speaking, the emission of seed by masturbation, nocturnal ejaculation, or interrupted intercourse is hardly different from the emission of seed in normal coitus resulting in conception. The difference between normal intercourse and masturbation, for example, is to be found elsewhere. Physiologically, the difference cannot be based on whether or not the seminal fluid has been lost.

When Onan spilled his seed in intercourse, he was punished by Yahweh because he had refused to generate an heir for his brother's widow; he refused to follow the Judaic law of the levirate (Deut. 25:5—10). Onan's disobedience, which brought on punishment, did not consist in the fact that "he spilled his seed upon the ground." This idea of the "sacred seminal fluid"—bearer of life

crease. The activity of these two substances works a
deep change in the uterine mucous and in the tonicity
of the cavernous muscle which is the uterus itself. Proliferation of the mucous, accumulation of glycogen, the
"sideration" of the uterine muscle tonicity—all this contributes to preparing the gestation organ for its eventual
function: the insertion of the egg, the growth of the
embryo and then of the fetus.

In the course of fecundation, the ovule fecundated by
one or two spermatozoa becomes imbedded in the uterine
wall, ordinarily quite far up and near one of the corners
of the cavity. Immediately the cyclic function of the
ovaries is suspended. The yellow body, or lutein, is
installed for a duration of about nine months, at the end
of which time the fetus is pushed out with its connected
membranes. When lactation ceases, the ovarian cycle
resumes its ordinary rhythm. In the female dog, for
example, this cyclic process occurs on the average of
twice during the year. Allowing fifteen years as the average life-span for the female dog, with fourteen years as
the normal duration of its genital life, this represents
about twenty-eight ovulations because the canine female
is not subject to the menopause.

The woman's cycle is completed in twenty-eight days.
If we set the average duration of the woman's genital life
at thirty-five, then, theoretically, there will be about 420
ovulations.

From this comparison alone it may be seen that the

woman's genital physiology, although in some ways comparable to that of females in the higher order of animals, is, withal, radically different. In the woman there is an ovarian proliferation completely out of proportion with the actual times and possibilities of gestation and nursing a child.

But there is also another equally important difference. In the female animal, the instinctive seeking for copulation is set in motion by the phenomenon of ovulation. This is the rutting period. The male animal's search for copulation is, in a very general way, unleashed by the rut of the female. Outside this period, however, the sexual instinct is dormant and is not manifested. Woman, for example (and this is something quite remarkable), is the only living "female" who undergoes coition during the time of gestation.[1] Strictly speaking, for her there is really no such thing as the rutting phenomenon. At the very most, certain women desire or welcome more frequent sexual relations during the days of their ovulation. In reality, however, this phenomenon has little importance.

It should be obvious, then, that human sexual desire is under the influence of something other than physiological factors. Extrapolating human behavior from animal

---

[1] In such domesticated animals as the dog, traces of aberration are discoverable in their sexual behavior. Is this "human contagion" or reflexes released by odors or other contributing causes which are not clear to us?

experimentation involves a great deal of naïveté. This tendency to oversimplify is, unfortunately, not always avoided by those who write on this subject.

In between the physiological and rational levels there is the whole universe of the "affective" psychic life which Freudian discoveries have bequeathed to scientific knowledge. This affective world will be the object of the following section of this book.

Since Ogino and Knaus completed their investigations some sixty years ago, the knowledge of female genital physiology has become much more exact. A woman, as everybody knows, can become pregnant only during a certain part of her ovarian cycle. The most likely time of pregnancy corresponds to that of ovulation which takes place halfway through the cycle. This is the rule for the average woman, but the precise moment of ovulation can vary widely from one woman to another. Rarely, however, does pregnancy occur before the eighth day or after the twentieth. It is very normal for each woman always to ovulate at the same stage in her cycle. Rather pronounced metabolic variations, entailing sex hormone activity, become quite accurately noticeable. At first, there are changes in the normal-temperature graph. If the temperature is taken each morning before the woman gets out of bed, it will show a slight dip at the moment of the follicle's bursting. Then there is an immediate increase of temperature which, until the end of the cycle, puts it slightly above the preceding level.

The methodical observation of this morning temperature allows (or would allow) most women to have sure knowledge of their own personal rhythm of fertility. Another equally valid way of detecting a very early sign of pregnancy is this: if the ovule is fertilized, there is no rise of temperature, and the "thermic plateau" of the second period does not occur.

In general, the bursting of the follicle is accompanied by a painful sensation that is both sharp and transitory, but difficult to locate precisely. Normally, it even escapes notice. However, if this pain is observed in relation to the thermic graph, it becomes significant and adds another element to what is already known.

Finally, in the hours preceding ovulation, a viscous substance, like the white of an egg, which blocks entry into the uterus, is expelled. If the woman pays any attention at all, she will be able to detect it. This is a third sign which, coupled with the two other signs, completes the data of experience.

We must also point out that the survival-duration of the non-fertilized ovule is rather brief—from twenty-four to thirty-six hours; however, the survival-duration of spermatozoa placed in the woman's genital tract is much longer and varies considerably. The average duration is four or five days, but it can go as long as from eight to ten days.

By way of a concrete example, if a woman who ovulates on the twelfth day of her cycle has sexual rela-

III

SOME MAIN POINTS OF PSYCHO-SEXUAL EVOLUTION

initiating self-reproduction does not, because of that, continue on in a less than normal life. Should the general term "aggressive instincts" be understood as those channelled powers which give assurance to the "need for existence," and should sexual instincts be understood as those which move the individual to share in the species' "need for existence," then it is at once clear that aggressive instincts *force* their subject to act, while sexual instincts, despite their periodic intensity, exercise no such force. It would be wrong to say that continence—the non-use of sex—brings on organic disorders.

If an inhibition (actually, the opposite of continence) in a man should cause difficulties, such difficulties are not of the bodily order; they are, rather, difficulties which are proper to the psychic, affective life which is man's specific kind of existence. This will be our next matter for discussion.

wants its own special—secret, if you will—world; and it wants full, not partial, citizenship in the adult world.

Hand in hand with the new approaches to others goes sexual awakening. Emotional drives, desires and the sexual sensations, which, in earlier childhood, existed in emotional subconsciousness, now burst into sharp consciousness, although they lack clearly defined form.

Surely ambivalence best characterizes young people at this stage. The adolescent is like the swimmer who has yet to take his first dive into the water, yet ambitions being a champion diver. Alone with his thoughts, the would-be diver summons his courage and ponders the techniques he will try. Before he knows it, there he is on the diving board. Standing there, he has the identical desire which moved him to take this first step, but now he is beset with fear. He has neved dived before. He knows now the vast difference between knowing and executing diving techniques. Now he finds himself backing away in dread, a dread brought on by the very desire that placed him on the diving board. There he stands, playing tug-o'-war all by himself. Such is the ambivalence of adolescence: a life desire which in its very expression brings on fear and aversion *simply because it is desire*.

Like the would-be diver, the adolescent wants to plunge into the adult world. His desire is related both to his need for living and to his sexual needs in a wide sense. Yet, from the point of view of actual experience, this adult world is an unknown factor. His desire has brought

him face-to-face with fear: Will he be accepted? Will he
be denied, brushed aside, even punished or emasculated?
Can he face the challenge of the world which he desires?
And there is also this consideration: his past life has not
given him the opportunity to evaluate himself realis-
tically. The obvious course of action, therefore, is to pre-
tend to hide the fear that he will be regarded as inept
and inferior. And in any discussion which involves his
own interests, he must have the final word; being wrong
would be intolerable.

Negatively stated, this comes down to saying that the
adolescent lacks that comfortable security which marked
the hidden period. The blossoming of his own complex
vital dynamism accounts, in a way, for the very turmoil
in the adolescent. Now, although adolescence is a later
and a different life-stage, still there is some parallel between the confusions experienced in adolescence and in
the first seven years. Both periods exhibit an uncertainty:
an uncertainty about the individual's relation with himself; an uncertainty about the individual's relation with
the other. The very effort to make advances in life is sur-
rounded with this incertitude, and this can only entail
certain regressive patterns of behavior. If no pathology
is involved, these patterns are transitory and of minor
importance.

When the little baby of one or two years finds itself in
a situation of what seems to be inescapable frustration—
the cause has nothing to do with our current concern—

it can do only one thing to bring temporary relief: it reverts to a past source of satisfaction. Now, sucking its thumb—more accurately, nursing its thumb—is not the real satisfaction desired by the baby at the moment, but it is a fairly good substitute, and it helps the baby to tolerate the situation somewhat better.

Clearly, such reaction is simply a return to earlier oral satisfaction. Yet, the object chosen for oral satisfaction is neither the object of its real and current desire nor is it the object (womb) of its old desire. But the illusion is there, and it is a transitory one; at least it lets the baby quiet down and go to sleep.

However, there is another side to this behavior. The thumb-sucking child suspends, for a time, all connection with its surroundings (and with what frustrates it) in order to seal itself off in a world that is almost wholly one of phantasy. In effect, the baby is no longer present to its surroundings; it has retreated into what we may call a dream world. Because at that moment he happens to have no satisfactory relation with the other (to the extent that we may speak of such at this level), he takes himself as the object of his desire in a sort of closed circuit. This behavior comes under the very common term, "auto-erotism."

Considerable analogy is to be found between the returns to autoerotism by the adolescent, on the one hand, and the child, on the other. Now since, in the normal course of events for the adolescent, genital sexuality has taken a commanding position and its concomitant sensual and emotional qualities now occupy consciousness, then these autoerotic recurrences must be assigned to the sex area. To put it bluntly, masturbation is adolescent thumbsucking. The adolescent's efforts to find his place in the real world bring on the doldrums, uncertainties and many forms of disquietude; these, in turn, bring on masturbation. To "locate" masturbation, in the case of the adolescent boy, we must point to the genital area itself; yet, with the adolescent girl, masturbation cannot be located so precisely, and it is, furthermore, more affective than sensual in character. Nonetheless, the basic significance of these returns to autoerotism is identical for all adolescents.

Finally, the first phase of adolescence is further characterized by what we may call the uni-sex reaction. Some writers choose to call this the homosexual phase, but, to my mind, this term causes entirely too much confusion.

At this stage in life, "dialogue" with children is unbearable for the adolescent; with adults, it is simply impossible; with members of the other sex—*the most other of others*—it is worse than impossible. Stirrings of what is literally anguish, vague fears of castration, deep-rooted helplessness to answer a simple question, and total panic make conversation with *the* boy or *the* girl an impossibility. The only dialogue possible for the adolescent is with himself, which is to say, with others of the same sex and age-bracket. And so we have the gangs—boy gangs and girl gangs, organized and otherwise—and their distinctive garb of leather jackets and the like.

Second Adolescence

Long before there was scientific understanding of sexuality, abstract principles regarding it had been formulated. It makes simple sense that there ought to be knowledge of just what autoerotism is before moral judgment is made concerning it.

The first impression one gets in studying the adolescent is that the really *important* thing is the matter of autoerotic practices (masturbation, for example). And this notion has been reinforced by a certain moralism which has its roots in taboos. It becomes necessary, then, to realize that these sexual "difficulties"—as we refer to them in all modesty—do not constitute the most obvious symptom in normal personality development. Why autoerotic acts are viewed as the most apparent symptom is easily explained: too many unenlightened people are obsessed with spotlighting this one symptom and with isolating it from its deep underlying causes, and this to the detriment of full understanding of the adolescent. Harm is done, both from the psychological and the spiritual points of view, by stressing unduly the importance of masturbation. Suppose, by analogy, the doctor were to treat the pimples rather than the measles. The absurdity here is that all attention is centered on the symptom, none on the sickness. By the same token, a good way *not* to help the adolescent overcome what some persist in regarding as a pathological condition rather than a normal crisis in personal development is to direct all concern to the symptom—regardless of its sexual character—rather than to the heart of the problem. Perhaps the tendency to spotlight the symptom of autoerotism in the adolescent is due in part to the fact that early awareness of genital sexuality is tied in with profound anguish.

The second step in adolescence is the step-by-step solving of the crisis. The subject enjoyed a temporary equilibrium as a child, and adolescence came along to upset it. Now the subject wants to establish a new equilibrium, a satisfactory and balanced relationship with himself and the other.

The *exact* time which marks the passing from the first to the second stage of adolescence cannot be chronologically determined. When something is set in motion, its beginning can be noted, at least to some extent; but, as the motion continues, it is not possible to pinpoint the various time-segments. And the reason is obvious: no stopping—no disparate time-segments—is a very attribute of evolution. If one were to examine the situation at a given *static* moment, so to speak, he would determine that change has taken place. He is in no position, however, to make a determination about the precise time of the transition from the first to second stages of adolescence.

The result is that, when we speak of successive stages in this second adolescence, we are assigning to these stages artificially divided segments of time. True, we shall get from successive observation points a good idea of stage following stage, but it will bear a poor resemblance to the real evolution going on. Language, which is the joining together of contiguous yet distinct words, is an unfair imprisonment of the concept and reality of evolution.

It may be said, in a general way, that the adolescent develops to the point of establishing intersubjective relationships and thus discovers his own personality. He will reach that point where he will have sufficient emotional stability to face the other and to assert himself as a person in the presence of those who have themselves arrived at this state.

And his relations with others will suffer no real harm for the fact that there still remain, in the deeper recesses of consciousness, those earlier reactions to the object desired, possessed, or rejected. He will have assumed sufficient independence in relation to the other to be psychologically suited for dialogue, strictly so called, whether that dialogue be important and lasting or of minor and momentary consequence.

Describing—and, perforce, it must be schematic—the development of the sexual side of personality gives a satisfactory grasp of the broad meaning of taking up the role of an adult. We should not lose sight of the fact that the sexual side is one side only, although most meaningful in making dialogue possible—the sex dialogue, that is.

In the beginning, the young boy discovers sexual attraction. It is, in its own way, both intense, yet lacking in clear outlines. Attraction for a girl is "timid," and it has no precise support, as though the subject did not yet dare set his desire on a really definite object. Erotic imaginings are evoked ("bad thoughts," in the moralist language of the taboo), are limited to incomplete but specifically feminine objects of curiosity. Parenthetically, it would be very interesting to have a better knowledge of how—before and at this stage of sexuality—the transition takes place from the womb-object for the child to the womb-object for the man.

Ambivalence, in the meaning earlier explained, has a tendency to calm down rather quickly, in the sense of breaking away from fear. Desire is developed and reaches a peak in imagination. The woman who occupies the youth's imagination is no longer "without a name" or "half-developed." Her face may represent someone encountered in real life or it may that of a film star. The relation, however, still remains on the level of the imaginary. At the very most, the adolescent relies on the help of pictures, pornographic or not, for arousal. The object of his desire is still the "woman of two dimensions."

As this development continues, there is now a desire for a real woman. Yet the woman of the youth's desire is still desired only as an *object;* at the very least, the relation to "the desired object" is still predominant, because this other object which confronts the youth is beyond him, so to speak; he is still too weak in his personal psychological security. Bit by bit, the tendency toward solitary masturbation is replaced by a desire for actual sexual relations with a partner "who would be only an object." Obviously a prostitute best fits this role. Once she has been paid, she can drop out of the picture. The difficulty is, however, that the relation with a prostitute is an anonymous, clearly false sort of thing.

In the meantime, the young girl herself is involved in her own "search period." When she meets a "square" or the "big man on campus," she, too, establishes a relation with the "object" alone, although she creates the illusion of a more human relation. This is flirtation time (in the "sensual" meaning of the word), or the time of transitory "crushes." In some instances, there are still traces of the masturbation type, although this gradually passes with time. The other person is experienced as a means of tension-relief or of satisfying desire.[2] There is no person-to-person relationship in which each person recognizes the other *as a person* with all his real qualities. In the case

[2] At least in the early stages of adolescence, mutual masturbation can occur between partners of the same sex. This does not mean a necessary deviation in the sexual orientation. Many adolescents have practiced this form of gratification and have grown up to be perfectly normal. On the other hand, some homosexuals never did engage in this action as adolescents.

of the young man, he is far from proving his virility. All he has done, actually, is to show that, in his present state, he is still unable to enter into a person-to-person relationship, and often for reasons other than sex.

Either as a result of the natural course of his development or because he has made another's acquaintance (the latter is more often the case), the young man arrives at this interpersonal relation. The other person is now looked upon as a person with whom a real-life relation is desirable. The sexual act now means fulfillment and introduction to a much wider world than his own; the sexual act means now a great deal more than a release from tension or a solitary pleasure, both desired for their own sakes. Erotism, in its new meaning, reveals deep person-to-person relationship, outside of which relationship it is nothing but a casual skimming over the surface of reality. In effect, this is to say that the normally developed young man is no longer at certain times inundated by the flood of his sexual desires, that he is becoming psychologically capable of continence due to the harmonious union of all his personal powers. All his powers are now polarized in the direction of the *person* he loves. The subject undergoing this "change of direction" in the sexual act usually regards it as normal progress and sees no need of any astonishment. However, this same change can cause uneasiness in a young man who has settled into the sexual behavior of an adolescent

tions the first two days, she runs little risk of becoming pregnant. The risks increase during the following days and up to the time of ovulation itself. There is no chance of fertility from forty-eight hours after ovulation—that is, on the fourteenth day—until the end of her menstruation. The phenomenon of a second, late ovulation, whether brought on by coition or not, is extremely rare.

Two reflections derive from these findings. The first, insistence on which seems needless, indicates that man's sexual life is not conducted, as with the animal, under the sole influence of instinct and physiological functions. Another quite different modal quality of being enters into play. This must, indeed, be called conscious and reflex, as is the case with all strictly human forms of behavior, no matter what they may be. In other words, moral life is not governed by physiology.

The second reflection, which is applicable to the animal, as well as to man, indicates that the sexual function, while calling into play intense and complex physiological activities, is not, for all that, something inescapable; it shows, furthermore, that sexual activity is not a prime necessity for the organism. We still encounter the widespread prejudice that intercourse brings a certain bloom to the woman by the "transfusion" of masculine hormones. Sperm is not the vehicle of hormones. The aftereffects of a sexual life must always be sought on the psychic level. It is entirely true, however, that pregnancy, with the rather long persistence of the luteum and all the physiological activity which pregnancy entails, is an important factor of fulfillment with regard to the female organism. This is true, provided that pregnancy is not repeated too often and that the physical and psychological conditions in which pregnancy progresses are sufficiently normal. Denying that some pregnancies are tragedies would be naïve in the same sense that it would be naïve to deny that normal motherhood redounds positively to the physiological well balanced condition of the woman.

Before leaving the physiological area, a final remark is in order.

In a very general and schematic manner, the needs of the living organism can be said to express and realize themselves by means of the vital dynamism of instincts. The only difference between the animal and man, but clearly an important difference, is this, that the instincts in man are "obscure" and radically ineffective as far as giving complete and exact direction to human behavior is concerned. Man's needs and the animal's are basically the same. Two such needs may be mentioned: first, the individual's need to assure and to defend its existence; secondly, the individual's need to share in the existence of the species. The second need is obviously impossible of assurance without the satisfaction of the first need: the dead simply do not share in reproduction. And, yet, the first need is not compromised if there is no fulfillment of the second need: the individual who is prevented from as though that were to be his normal state. It is by no means uncommon for young boys, arriving at maturity, to become disturbed because they no longer experience pressing sexual desires; in fact, some of them begin to worry that they may be impotent. The real difficulty faced in explaining the significance of this change is that the young man was really expecting something else: namely, meeting up with a woman-subject of whom he is still somewhat fearful because this will mean a change in his life.

Integration of the Past Life

Everybody knows that the early days of adolescence are intended to be the privileged age of dreaming, and there is more significance in this than first meets the eye. No longer is there question of that world of phantasy which the child creates as its playground. The young man no longer is happy merely to convert a soap box on roller skates into a sports car or limousine. His playing days are over, and now he wants to dream by himself, letting his imagination race over subjects that are completely personal, yet world-wide in scope. The imaginary something which he builds up is *himself-made-real*. All the remnants of his primitive struggles and of the world of phantasy form the raw material for this build-up. This is the struggle undertaken by the subject to thrust himself into the real world as he sees it, that is, to find a place for himself where he can deal successfully with adults.

At the same time, these dreams are primarily a form of escapism. The chief relations in the life of the adolescent are those of family and school, relations which become painfully unsatisfactory and entirely too confining. He wants to have the relations of an adult with other adults, but such relations are still unattainable, and they are marked by a twofold tension. In consequence, he runs away from this tension into a world of phantasy, and, while this world means something from the sexual angle, it nevertheless has its development in general fields of activity.

The mark of this imaginative life is its timelessness. The young boy sees himself as an explorer; the young girl, a princess. But there is a stability in the world as these young people create it. There is a timelessness about it, a state of motionless perfection. Only gradually will this imagination, as a flight into dreamland, change into creative imagination. The dream-role will become one of making plans. The significance to be noted here is that the subject will gradually succumb to the possibility of his becoming part of a time-world that is real and experienced as such, of becoming a part of "existential time" by finding himself woven into it for good. In other words, by his ability to take his place in real relations with adults, the *others* (whether from the point of view of sexuality or of aggressiveness), he accepts himself, so to speak, as a subject of duration.

Real life leads on to death. Never before, in its own inner world, had the child been disturbed by prospects of death, and death meant nothing to him except as an occasional, transitory fear. For the adolescent, however, the realization that death is a reality is, perhaps, his most disquieting problem. Entering adulthood means becoming part of the active world of men. His new life is not static, as in a dream; it moves on through time and toward inevitable death, and this new adult profoundly realizes it as his personal and inescapable destiny.

Very few young people can plan anything. Plans do not arouse emotions. Young people spring from their dreamworld directly into action without reflection. This is the real meaning behind vandalism and juvenile delinquency. Remaining in their play-world, adolescents find the transition into real adult life just too much for them. "What do you think you'll be like in ten years?" means literally nothing to them. Insecure emotionally, they cannot be reached and really motivated by such a question. Every adolescent needs all the help and understanding he can get from sympathetic adults, so that he may gradually find his own way in the adult social world.

This "investiture of personal death" occurs on a much deeper level than that of conscious reflection, but it necessarily ends in conscious expression. At the end of his development, the adolescent, by way of sublimation, enters symbolically into the womb of the human community, and he or she enters as man or as woman. This new situation resolves his primitive anguish, but it also confronts the adolescent with the basic contradiction of his being which has now become a very distinct personal existence. Being able to say "I" means becoming conscious of self (as stable and definitive), and it also implies an involvement aimed at a separation from men and the world. The older I become, the more I am aware *that* I am and *who* I am. Yet, at the same time that I enrich my person, I grow old and am faced with the consummation of something. This word "consummation" is very ambiguous, for it means both end and beginning. When the artist has consummated his work, he has terminated, "accomplished," realized it—and then the contemplation of his work begins.

That stage at which the adolescent becomes conscious of time that moves onward toward death coincides with the integration of his sexuality, for his sexuality has now successfully passed through its probationary period. Here, once more, occurs that strange aspect of the sexual reality which we noted at the beginning. On the human level, the "paradox" of sexuality as giver of life and revealer of individual death is disclosed by man's questioning consciousness. Therein is found the entire man, from the most remote and obscure zones of his emotional life all the way up to his most refined spiritual reflections.

At the close of these considerations on adolescent sex-

uality, proper emphasis should be given to certain pre-
dictable questions.

First, is adolescent masturbation a normal and unavoidable occurrence or, on the contrary, is it something really
pathological, although (at least in normal development)
of minor importance?

At the risk of being overly schematic, the distinction
must be made between what can be called accidental and
habitual masturbation.

Any boy at all, from time to time and at irregular intervals, can find himself overcome with passion, with the
result that he will seek solitary sexual pleasure. In the
normal course of his development, he will survive this
critical period in short order and without too much difficulty. This autoerotism then diminishes and finally disappears. All this is entirely normal. Nocturnal emissions
again take place normally, according to their basically
irregular rhythm.

Masturbation is practiced with extreme frequency (95
to 98 per cent of adolescents have engaged in this practice, according to different statistics), almost as a regular
habit. This means engaging in masturbation one or more
times a week over periods which vary from person to
person, from a few months to a few years. In this sense,
masturbation is a different problem altogether. A "fixa-
tion" sets in at a critical time, and it does not pass away.
This kind of abnormal tardiness in getting rid of autoerotic regression can, however, have extremely variable

meanings. It can range simply from the adolescent encountering some difficulty (with no really neurotic connotation) right up to seriously pathological conditions of the personality, either in the restricted sphere of sexuality or in other ranges of expression. At any rate, the habit of masturbation is not alarming in itself. It is merely a symptom, and there are other symptoms of "adaptation-sicknesses" which are more important.

Obviously, education is very important. A youth should grow up in a satisfying emotional atmosphere, receive sex instruction that is clear and suited to his age, and develop an outlook freed, as far as possible, both from taboo and "moralistic pan-sexualism." Under such conditions, the adolescent will very likely have the fewest possible difficulties and will not be bogged down very long in the closed circle of a habit that must be overcome.

For further sexual development, especially in married life, the presence or absence during adolescence of this "imperfection" of masturbation (especially if it be of long standing) is not a wholly indifferent matter. This habit can handicap adaptation to sexual life in marriage by causing either the continuation or fresh outbreaks of auto-erotic tendencies which, in turn, can have unfortunate effects on intercourse and on the development of a wholesome outlook on sexual desire.

Some adolescents do not know how to break the masturbation habit. Parents, educators, and moral or medical counselors should realize that, except for a few pathological cases, they can help these young people only by assisting them in developing some other absorbing interest. The adolescent must be made to understand that his habit is but the after-effect of something else: the cause may be a difficulty in adaptation or the result of something entirely other than sexuality, properly so called. By assuming his place in the adult world, the adolescent will overcome this habit and witness the end of his autoerotic regression.

What has been said here is also applicable to many of the "sexual difficulties" in married life. Most of the time, the source of these difficulties is not to be sought on the level of genital sexuality (because it is not clear that their nature is physiological). These troubles generally originate not in the sexual life, properly so called, but rather in the complexity of emotional and psychological relationships that exist between the two married parties.

IV

THE MEANING FOR MAN
OF GENITAL SEXUALITY

FOR THE DISCUSSION of genital sexuality in adults (something always relative), some few considerations are necessary. These will help clarify certain behavior-patterns in their specifically human and spiritual dimension. A new dynamic orientation of sexual behavior is disclosed by information derived from the sciences, especially psychology, and by the help of reflection on the data of experience and research alone. This might almost be called a "natural ethics," were the term not so ambiguous in current discussions.

Man alone decides how he should behave, and this immediately distinguishes him from all other living creatures. He is able to avail himself of those guidelines provided to him by the advance of science and a modern philosophy that is not departmentalized into aprioristic and abstract categories.

Because some "philosophic systems" have degenerated into mere *systems* with all the *status quo* that term implies; they are no longer wellsprings of new discoveries. Such philosophies are based on outdated scientific knowledge and have become sterile, with consequent loss of value. Thus, scholastic philosophy has betrayed the dynamic ferment injected into it by its founder, and it may be stated that the powerful personality of St. Thomas would scarcely recognize itself in modern Thomism.

The problem must, therefore, be approached otherwise. The answer is to be found in very humble work, in constant recourse to the observable world of reality and in whatever will unfailingly widen the course of research.

The Specific Nature of Human Sexuality

In the light of the emotional development of the personality, we have seen that, ideally, the integration and ordering of man's fundamental powers is the minimal requirement of interpersonal relations. With regard to sexuality, it means the ability to establish a true marriage-relationship, one desired as such. This capacity further implies, by a seeming paradox, the possibility of even going beyond the married state. This would entail establishing relations of another order, relations wider in scope and affording an equally genuine emotional expansion. Celibacy, even though quite often the result of an inhibition (in the technical meaning of that word), can be the expression of unusual maturity and, therefore, the result of a definitely positive choice.

Let us suppose the case of a man and woman who, under the best of conditions, are living a married life. What can be the meaning of their genital sexual relations, properly so called?

Contrary to what takes place in the animal, this meaning is twofold, from the very fact of "retirement" and of "transcending the world" which makes man *present to* and in dialogue with another. In animal coitus, the biological function of reproduction is expressed. In human coitus there is an altogether different dimension, namely, that of the encounter of two questioning consciousnesses whose roles are determined in a way proper to each.

The biological function is the same; the sexual act sets in operation a specialized physiological system of which the differentiated structuration and functioning are *oriented* toward reproduction. In my opinion, it would be an error in philosophic method to forget that the exercise of the genital function "has something to do" with fecundity, even if conception does not take place or cannot take place.

From the existential point of view, however, it is quite clear that something else takes place besides the biological activity of the couple. On the level that is most specifically human (psychological and spiritual), the sexual union is a very special kind of encounter.

Married life is a dialogue that goes on unceasingly. It moves forward indefinitely in search for harmony—a harmony that is always relative but, ideally at least, one that is increasingly experienced by the two parties. This dialogue continues even during long absences and the daily separations attendant upon concrete existence, and it unfolds on very different plateaus of married life. Every instance of give-and-take, even the seemingly trivial, contributes to success in the married relation: use of the bathroom, establishing some order for the thousand and one details of everyday life, choosing a car—all these constitute intimate contact that is often jarring, that demands of each party an agreeableness for the other, one that promises to become ever more perfect. These very humdrum daily contacts, which seem to be of such little and fleeting importance, may well be the most meaningful expression of the married relation. Given this relation properly established, everything falls into place very nicely, and harmony is achieved without one word being spoken. Mutual understanding goes beyond words. However, when the fundamental relation is strained (for reasons that are often not clear), a harsh disagreement breaks out over some such a detail as where to place a piece of furniture. The tragedy of some marriages results from the inability to pinpoint and to settle the underlying cause of these quarrels over trivialities. Something evidently is wrong, but just what is wrong is not clear.

On an entirely different level, there are the strictly personal conversations wherein the couple share with one another those areas of the self that are most personal: thoughts, memories, anxieties, doubts—in a word, everything in the conscious self that can be shared with another.

The sexual encounter must be fitted into this entire marital context and in dependence on this context as well as on the quality of the intersubjective relation itself and the means of intensifying it.

The Intersubjective Relation in General

In order to put the true sexual encounter in proper perspective, we must now briefly consider the cause of every successful relation between persons. The principle is very simple, but its realization is often very difficult. In every life-situation, in which a relation has been established, there is a question of each one's receiving and recognizing the other in his personal reality and dimensions, in his own little world, and in what he asks, if only to tell him that his request is out of the question.

I happen to be rushing down the street to keep an appointment. Someone approaches me and asks directions to a nearby place of business. From my part, a "welcome" is shown this stranger if I give the impression that I find what is happening wholly natural. And whether he seems pleasant or not doesn't show in my attitude. If I don't know the address, I tell him as pleasantly as I can. On his part, the "welcome" consists in causing me the least possible inconvenience because he senses that I am in a hurry.

This simple example shows that there are countless numbers of every kind of human encounter. Being kind is not enough for the success of a relation. We can be kind because we want to make a good impression, want people to talk flatteringly about us, and not because the other is an existing person. Some forms of kindness succeed in alienating better than outright rejection of another.

Because of the thousand and one nuances involved in living relations, no exact and complete success formula may be given. The following example may give a somewhat better understanding of the extent of the requirements in living a relation, particularly where persons are involved more deeply and lastingly than in the casual encounter discussed above.

I have a close friend. We exchange confidences and are fully honest and open with each another. However, in his closely knit family circle there is an elderly maiden aunt who irritates me no end. She arouses aversions in me right down to the depths of my emotional life, and I can't overcome my feelings. In some way or other, these feelings are rooted in conflicts of my own childhood that were never resolved. In technical—perhaps disputable—terms, although I show this aunt all the amenities, she arouses a harsh negative transfer in me. I should love to annihilate this woman, especially since she means nothing to me. This is pure defense mechanism.

My friend thinks a great deal of his aunt, and certainly she doesn't arouse in him the aversions I experience. At her age, she may be somewhat silly and irritating, but her nephew probably loves her. My own negative transfer and urge to get rid of the aunt lead me to minimize my friend's relation to his aunt. Now if, unwittingly or unguardedly, I take measures to prevent his own positive relationship with his aunt, then a harmful note is subtly entering my relationship with her nephew. No matter how closely he and I are united in dialogue, deep in his consciousness is the idea that I tried to cut him off from a dimension that is meaningful to him. In his own private world, he will not feel *wholly* recognized; he will feel reduced to only those dimensions that please me. Gradually and inevitably, our friendship will cool and head-on clashes over trivialities will likely occur.

A single word of caution, lest anyone become too complacent about his relations to others. The mother-in-law is a problem for all seasons.

The Two Meanings of Human Sexuality

Sexual intercourse has an altogether special complexity for the reason that it involves a level below that open to consciousness. Here, only some aspects of this complexity can be suggested.

The first word coming to mind is mutual pleasure or, better, mutual sensual pleasure: to give sensual pleasure to the other and to receive sensual pleasure from the other—this, in a word, is the apparent ideal of the sexual exchange. The sexual exchange, therefore, is an exquisite expression of the whole existential relation of two beings in love with one another.

What exactly is this pleasure? The answer is not so simple. In the case of the woman, this pleasure may even reach an actual loss of consciousness. It rarely takes this form with men, but sometimes it does cause what can be called a "conditional disappearance of all contingency." In some places, popular language speaks of the "little death." If death be understood as being taken suddenly and violently out of the contingencies of time, then there is no paradox in saying that sexual pleasure does unquestionably involve a kind of "death," one mutually asked for and given.

At the same time, sexual pleasure gives the transitory but emotion-charged experience of a "blending" of the man and woman by virtue of the penetration itself. It is fusion which is not confusion, but a "distinguishing unity" which is both vitally intense and, at root, insufficient. I do not believe it paradoxical to say that "the act of love" brings to symbolic reality, on the level of the emotional experience, an "enticement" to unity of the two beings, together with the deep-rooted ambivalence involved in the intensity and radical illusion of its total insufficiency. In the unconscious psychological background, more or less sublimated, there is always to be found the dialectic that brings about anguish as we have described it in the first part of this work.

On the other hand, the voluptuous and emotional intensity is short. A return to time and to the "separation" follows it, namely, a return to the never satisfied quest of a total and "interior" presence of the other. On completion of the sexual act, a vastly complex psychological world opens up. And, while it implies a "bliss of grateful recognition," the nostalgic longing for what cannot be attained is never absent. Here again, the most primordial and obscure psychological world is involved. The man who withdraws from his wife after intercourse sees the wilting of an organ which "falls," and he has entered

upon his own existence and *his experience,* however
obscure it may be, by being cast out and "cut off" from
the same void.

The sexual encounter is actually a very ambivalent reality and it would be a complete oversimplification to reduce it to the mere idea of pleasure superficially understood. Besides, is not every "pleasure" the experiencing
of insufficiency and the ever-welling desire for something else?

The sexual encounter is a violent and lived-through
experience of an inexpressible unity, but one destined for
frustration, as though true unity were unrealizable in
this way. The encounter is a violent and lived-through
experience of a mutual exit from time and things con-
tingent (the word "ecstasy" is, doubtlessly, inadequate).
At the same time, it is an experience of an exit which
"comes to a halt," namely, one which does not succeed
in eluding time. Beyond question, the sexual encounter
is an experience lived in the spontaneous registers of the
human condition, one which reaches out farthest toward
the bursting of the infinite without ever arriving at its
goal.

Some "Situations"

The human sexual act, as we have described it, has
two levels of meaning, therefore: one, this very vast,

vehement, and complex quality of the interpersonal encounter found in the relation of the couple; secondly, genital fecundity.

These two meanings, however, are not always and of necessity present at the same time. This depends on the concrete, existential situations of the two parties. The clearest explanation of the matter will be found in a more detailed study of various possible situations.

By way of example, consider a couple in which the wife has passed the menopause, that is, she is now permanently sterile. In their sexual relations, this couple is concerned with only one of the two meanings of the sexual encounter; fecundity is out of the question. The sexual act means only the expression of their specific interpersonal relation in its twofold aspect: coitus will be a means of deepening their relation and, at the same time, of becoming more keenly aware that, deep down, the act of sexual relation is not enough. Gradually this will lead to an abstention-attitude with regard to intercourse. Yet, that certain relativity of desire which precedes and accompanies sexual relations will enable them to discover a love that goes beyond the sexual, a love that is deeper, more engrossing, literally inexpressible.

A different case is that of a younger married couple of thirty to thirty-five years of age. Both meanings of the sexual act are possible for them. Fecundity, however, is meaningful only at intervals. From a few days after ovulation up to the following menstruation, fecund-

ity is practically impossible for them. Before ovulation, it
is possible and even becomes increasingly more probable
ten or eleven days after menstruation begins. During the
interval of physiological sterility, this young couple is
in a situation which, though only temporary for them,
is almost identical with the position of the older couple.
In other words, if the wife in this case knew anything
positive about her cycle's regularity, she and her husband could, theoretically and ideally, "act out" both
meanings of their sexual relations. Pertinent to this, of
course, are their moral choice and the way they get along
together in their home life. Should the couple decide not
to have children for a time—both a reasonable and necessary control of fecundity—they might, among other
things, simply abstain from sexual intercourse throughout
the cycle's fertile period. By their mutual agreement
to space their marital relations, the position of this couple
is somewhat one of "transcending" their experiment
rather than one of being bogged down or limited by
habit (which is often called "hygienic," but which is
really both false and somewhat shocking). This couple,
then, is in a good position to continue the search for that
unity which can only be called spiritual—although this
word is ambiguous enough to carry both inaccurate and
distorted meanings.

  The third case concerns a couple at the time of the wife's
fertile period. They have decided not to have children,

at least for the time being; yet they continue to have sexual relations. To enjoy their intimacy and also to frustrate fecundity, they use an artificial contraceptive device. Or, too, they may interrupt the sexual act so that the sperm does not reach its natural destination.

There is a decided kind of incoherence, so to speak, in this behavior. Anyone would be inclined to think that, if a person does not want to do something, then the logical thing is simply to refrain from doing it. Certainly this makes more sense than to begin an action and then, by one's whole attitude, deny that same action by interruption. The behavior of this couple reflects either the absence of moral judgments or else a lack of emotional maturity on the part of either or both husband and wife. If we consider the couple from this second perspective, then we must conclude that they never rose above the level of genital sexuality because of difficulties of adaptation and progress.

Viewing this same couple's behavior from the angle of the demands involved in every interpersonal relationship, the practice of contraception betrays a weakness, an imperfection, a relative restriction. At the very moment the husband enters into sexual relations, he is related to a wife who is not merely a woman, but a potential mother. And it is this very existential dimension (both in its physiological and psychological nature) which he is summoning into being by the act of sexual intercourse. Yet, at the very instant in which he invites this dimension into being, he is denying the invitation by forbidding its culmination. The attitude of the wife is no different because she offers herself to a potential father, then proceeds to forbid potentiality to become actuality. In all sexual relations that involve contraception, something is cut away from this "total receptive welcome of the other" in all its actual existential dimensions.

The negative character assigned to this kind of marital sexuality is rarely recognized by the couple, and even more rarely is it intended. The fact remains that this character is inherent in the act itself. And the further fact is that such couples—when their marital relations are subjected to clinical study—often do sense a thwarting, an insufficiency, a kind of disorder in their own behavior. It is important to indicate here that when a couple, despite its finest intentions and strongest efforts, is unable to overcome the habit of contraception, very commonly this is due to some defect or lack in the psychological order rather than on the level of genital sexuality.

As a result of some rather recent findings in the fields of biology and pharmaco-dynamics, synthetic products are now available. Simply by ingesting one of these products, a woman is able to block the normal course of her ovarian cycle by hormonal means. When taken at a certain point in the cycle, these products prevent the formation of the follicle and impede ovulation. Given such discoveries, the problem of artificial physiological sterility faces us.

Even more recently efforts have been made to produce some chemical substance capable of delaying, for a period of time, the formation of spermatazoa in the male. A great deal remains to be learned about spermatogenesis, the result being that these studies have come to a halt for the time being.

Married people today, therefore, have at their disposal the power to effect a state of real physiological sterility, the duration of which varies. It is to be hoped, as a caution, that women, particularly young women, will avail themselves of these chemical products only under the advice of their physician. These products are by no means free from dangerous side-effects.

Despite the physical differences between these more recent products and those developed in years past, the intent of contraception remains. Certainly their development has no bearing on the problem of human sexuality itself. That problem remains always the way in which a man and a woman, committed to each other in a marriage relationship, live out or do not live out the twofold meaning of marital sexual life, properly so called.

The Sexual Act Is a "Social" Act

No matter how primitive or advanced its cultural content, every civilization has included, as expressive of its own human community, a rite which is of fundamentally social, religious or magical significance: *institutional mar-*

riage. Every civilization has been deeply concerned, within the social context, about the stability of the relationship between this man and that woman, or between this man and those women (polygamy), or between these women and that man (polyandry). And sexual commitment has been regarded, more or less explicitly, as the special characteristic of this relationship. Nor has the importance attached to a stable marriage been due to some *a priori* principle so much as to the very down-to-earth fact that groups of people living together must be organically welded.

The sexual encounter between a man and a woman will, on reflection, be revealed as a social act in the deepest meaning of that term. Sexual union is the actuating of the power of begetting children; in other words, the sexual act opens the way for a third person on the scene. No longer does the world exist for two people and their mutual tenderness; now, as a result of sexual union, there is a new world opening up, a world for three people, a world with innumerable new relationships. Let lovers embrace in the most tender way, and but two people are affected; but, when they enter into sexual relations, a third dimension is added as a possibility. This suffices to create a social situation and to link the man and the woman as a unit with the society in which they live.

Modern psychology explains the social character of fertility more methodically than our own observations and reflections. In broad outline, it is enough to recall that emotional security is the very first requisite for the child's normal development. The child is given the earliest assurance of its security in the unspoken language of the mother's attitudes, of her smiles and contentment, of the even rhythm of her life. Unless the mother herself is secure, no emotional security can be transferred to her child. And the mother, in turn, cannot be really secure unless she is recognized for what she is in the concrete situation and in the demands which the situation places upon her. The material and practical considerations of the mother's situation cannot be ignored, but they must be viewed within the surrounding human context. It is essential that the mother be known in relation to a father who is "sociologically identifiable," someone who, by his sexual union with her, establishes the mother in the fullness of her life. When a man and woman claim the right to sexual union, it is not too much to say that, for the greater success of the entire human enterprise, the human social context has a right to speak out in recognizing as its own and to incorporate the new subjects brought into being by marriage.

This really is the very basis of marriage as an institution, and it matters nothing whether marriage, as an institution, be regarded within the context of a tribe in remotest antiquity or within the context of the universal Church, entry into the Mystical Body included.

The very many cases of emotional imbalance, disturbed character and truly neurotic disorders among people who have grown up under abnormal circumstances are striking proofs, in a negative way, of the need of well-adjusted parents. A child will weather the Oedipus crisis only within a network of human familial relations well-integrated with the human context. And the same is true for the adolescence crisis.

It is a curious fact that the specifically sexual relationship, which normally calls for the highest secrecy—as if the world and all its happenings were inconsequential —is the very relationship which involves, in its infinite complexity, almost the entire network of human relationships. There is no outcry at the sight of a man and woman embracing publicly, but imagine the indignation at the performance of sexual union in public. For what a man and woman live through in the sexual act is far too important, far too solemn; in fact, it involves the whole mystery of life and death to the fullest extent; in a word, everybody is affected by it.

The Sexed and the Sexual

Consider this case of a man, forty years old, married, and a father. In great secrecy and embarrassment, he comes for advice. Two reasons impel him to come. As he discloses the reasons, this man shows that he is at least vaguely aware that the reasons are interwined. First of all, he is timid; secondly, he cannot refrain from what is, in his own judgment, both excessive and disordered sexual activity. In addition to sexual relations with his wife, he visits prostitutes several times a month.

By a somewhat closer scrutiny of this man's timidity and as a result of encouraging him to explain himself freely, it becomes clear that his real problem, in all his human relations, is to reach a point where he can be convinced of his own manliness. By dint of hard, even painful, labor he has brought himself to a point of some professional success, even though in his own field of competence he has always been afraid of being victimized. He has never really been at ease in giving orders to men of his own age, particularly to rough, tough laborers. He describes his wife as a superior type and, even while he protests his love for her, he confesses to a feeling of inferiority in their relationship. In fact, he has always been seeking a motherly protection from her, with the consequence that mutual understanding has suffered.

This subject is unable to establish *fully sexed* relationships. Everything that occurred in his disturbed existence was overshadowed by the fact that he was unrecognized as a man, even in his own estimation. And yet, this man had frequent sexual relations, more, in fact, than he cared to have. His reason for seeking advice was to acquire sexual self-control.

In a second case the subject is somewhat more of a

problem, He, too, is forty years old and a successful businessman, but he has never married. He has a real facility in getting along with others, both men and women, and there have been few real disagreements in his life contacts.

However, this man is inwardly torn because he has led a homosexual life ever since adolescence. No one knows his secret; in fact, the only surprise among this subject's friends is that he has never married. He cannot pinpoint his reluctance to marry, save that it would upset his entire pattern of living.

This man's sex life is reducible to occasional masturbation and a few stealthily arranged, invariably unsatisfying encounters with other homosexuals. The bitterness of his current situation and the prospect of a lonely life ahead have brought the subject in for advice. At the same time, he is not convinced that he really wants to reform.

Here, then, is a person who has attained sexed relations of uncertain satisfaction. In his everyday living he has the outlook of a man, and only a practiced psychologist would be able to detect that everything is not really what meets the eye. He is wholly impotent when it comes to normal sex relations, and his few earlier attempts have only reinforced his inadequacy. By his own admission, the best this subject has been able to do is to reduce harm to himself by spacing out his surrenders to his erotic impulses.

These two real-life cases highlight the difference between sexed and sexual relations. In the first case, the subject is fully capable of sexual relations, but has not arrived at the stage of sexed relations. In the second case, the subject reached the point of sexed relations, but is wholly apathetic regarding sexual relations.

Of the two cases, the homosexual is obviously the more unusual. Generally speaking, the homosexual has difficulties in relations other than sex and finds it troublesome to become part of the social whole. But this particular subject, who happens to be very talented and seems to have benefited from sound psychological training, appears to have resolved his problem rather early in life. He discovered his impotency for normal sexual relations during his adolescence, then set about to compensate for the lack in his life by establishing relations of another order—studies, social activities, cultural interests—in which his talents have blossomed. He has succeeded in developing his emotional makeup in order to go beyond himself as much as possible, and he has literally concealed his sexual neurosis. In fact, this subject reached the point where the question may be asked whether it would be the wrong thing for him, in his precise situation and at his age, to undergo psychoanalysis.

The first of the two cases is more commonplace. The emotional dissatisfaction of this subject is more general, more diffuse, and not properly identified by the subject himself. He never succeeds in learning just what is wrong; in consequence, he never confronts his difficulty to resolve it once and for all. His general attitude remains that of the adolescent; he has never really grown up. His inability to establish sexed relations takes its toll, in spite of himself, in his compulsive search for relations that are still quite masturbatory and in which his sexed partner is reduced to the state of anonymity.

A third and much more neurotic type of this emotional inadequacy is the Don Juan. Unceasingly in search of a relationship that is inevitably bungled, ever in headlong pursuit of what turns out to be second rate, the Don Juan type is clear manifestation of a deep, existential uneasiness.

Generally speaking, it may be said that the more successfully a person arrives at *sexed* relations, the less dependent he is on erotic drives and on his phantasmal and imaginary world. Furthermore, he is better capable of abstaining from sexual relations; he has reasons for doing so.

What is most surprising is that the second subject in the three cases we have considered—a subject so very disturbed in the development of his instinct—is nonetheless successful, for good or ill, in assuming a stance with regard to his sexed relations. The sublimation of even an abnormal situation—a very primitive one—is, therefore, relatively possible. This, of course, introduces the special problems of the profound meaning and the relativity of the genital and erotic sexual invert.

V

THE TEACHING OF JUDAEO-CHRISTIAN REVELATION CONCERNING SEXUALITY

Lights

The forward march of science is really rather new in the
history of humanity, thanks to the giant strides it has
taken in the last 150 years. It has given man a new
awareness of his nature and of the dynamism of the universe. As a consequence, the prevailing philosophical
mentality, so shot through with rationalism, has been
seriously called into question. At the very heart of this
new awareness is sexuality, as known in its existential
reality, and it is sexuality which raises the fundamental
question of relation (to others) as the only question, in
the countless ways it manifests itself, that is of vital concern to us. This simple fact demonstrates the importance

of the upheaval destined to take place in the world of thought when nominalism, which ignores or denies the relation (of one reality to another), is recognized for its subtle infiltration.

A single example will suffice. A given philosophy studies the human act, neatly dissects it into very exact stages or definite points, makes fine distinctions among deliberation, choice, decision, and the like; then follows reflection on what makes up the human act, what constitutes its finality, what is its worth with respect to the good. All this thought, ingenious as it may be in its precisions, fails completely to take into account, *as a starting point,* that the human act has existence only as a *relation to the other,* no matter what the level of consciousness may be. Some of the jargon in scholastic philosophy—although the vehicle of some magnificently *exact* ideas—appears, by this very fact, to be henceforth indefensible. In its extreme form and in the long run, it will establish a veritable prison because this way of thinking allows for only the abstract, isolated subject, and "the other" is really absent from that subject.

Irreconcilability is clearly inevitable between those who adhere to ancient systems of thought and those who, principally following upon Freudian discoveries, recognize the lack of realism in "the perennial philosophy." Failure to see the mystery of sexuality at both the center and the origin of all possible reflection explains the lack of realism in older systems of thought.

We must be aware and acknowledge, however, that this new reflection, this modern dimension in thought, cannot be extended too far if complete and fully satisfying clarification is wanted. It is a road leading into a dense forest, and we can easily become lost in questions to which there is no reply, most particularly with regard to the definitive meaning of the sexual mystery.

It will be of interest, therefore, to investigate what is to be learned about sexuality from sources of knowledge other than science. In other words, given the situation in which modern man has been able to open up certain areas, deep within himself and never before explored, the question arises as to whether someone other than man may have something to say in answer to the really puzzling question as to whither the reality of sexuality leads and as to the limits of its own proper dimensions?

The Judaeo-Christian revelation is the word of this Someone whom men agree on calling "God" (although the term is so ambiguous and so confusing that we hesitate to use it). Reflection on what revelation by this Other can teach about sexuality will be interesting, and all the more so because, from the viewpoint of this revelation, the sexual reality is equally fundamental and the beginning of all (Genesis 1 and 2).

In these few pages there can obviously be no exhaustive treatment of the subject. We can try to sketch only certain essential topics. At the same time, we shall make every effort to present this outline according to perspectives freed from the subtle infiltration of scholastic and nominalistic thought, both of which still paralyze so much of this type of work.

The "Separation" from Transcendence

Unique to the Judaeo-Christian revelation is the fact that the One speaking declares solemnly that he is transcendent, utterly above and beyond all created being. He has nothing in common with man. He is the Unknowable, the Unapproachable; He is so much Other that the "secret of his thought and plans" is infinitely beyond anything which human thought can reach (Job). In addressing Abraham, inaugurating his dialogue with the whole of humanity through the Jewish people, the first thing which the One speaking does is to establish with precision—as a preamble, so to speak—this fundamental separation. Until that point in human history, men had fashioned their own gods. No matter how powerful these gods, they remained always within a human pattern. Man's accomplishment in establishing gods and a hierarchical order among the gods is a most important accomplishment for the reason that his efforts reveal a glimpsing of some higher power, one outside himself, a higher world beyond his own. With revelation, however, all this has changed and, from this day forward, Someone is present who is not an imaginary being and who can never be described in human terms. His name, given to Moses as a sign of recognition, is profoundly mysterious. The name signifies both the absolute reality of existence as well as the fact that the secret of his existence cannot be humanly probed. His name means "I am who am," but it also means "I am who am and whom you cannot know."

In a word, Yahweh told men, "You are not I, and I am not you." This is, furthermore, an assurance of man's true existence, together with the fullness of joy proper to it and the assurance which man needs. Above all, Yahweh's words to man place him at that essential distance which alone permits of a true relation.

I can have genuine consciousness of myself as a real, unique, distinct subject only to the degree in which I am aware that I am not the other. It must here be noted that this need of distance in accordance with the evidence adduced, this need of distance—separation— is the basic character of psychological evolution. Step by step, the child becomes conscious of himself through a succession of separations involved in "symbolic castration." By his awareness that he *is not* his mother, that he is not part of her, that he *is not* "the object" of his father, that he is alone, by himself, with all the opposing tension implied by this situation—in a word, by taking up his position *at a distance*—the child comes to be himself with the minimal amount of security sufficient for carrying on his life.

Through an intricate succession of separations, from

the time of the child's birth, the parents bring it about that the child assumes its own existence by separating it from themselves. Yahweh, the Creator, separates his conscious creature by the infinite distance of His own transcendence; and *that is what makes the creature exist.* Man, in his contingency, can become conscious of fully existing only by awareness of himself *as a creature,* namely, as not being that Absolute Existent which causes him to come into being from nothing.

The Relation

The Jewish people were somewhat unique for their keen awareness of the divine transcendence. Their ritual acts went so far that they strike the observer as verging on magic. Yet, their ritual really had a deep meaning of religious consciousness. The name Yahweh was never uttered. People spoke of his "arm" or used other forms of circumlocution. Even the consonants of his name were written backwards, lest readers dare pronounce them.

As God's word was made known through continuing revelation, it became clearer and clearer to human understanding. The transcendent and monotheistic "bloc" gradually brought to light different aspects of itself, as though from a strange inner life-principle. At first, the "wisdom" of Yahweh was spoken of, as if it were a reality distinct from Yahweh in its action (Proverbs 8).

And the word went out of "someone who will come," of him "who will save the people" (and, implicitly, the entire human race). Originally there was something strange and almost contradictory about the figure of this "expected," this "desired." At one time he is a king; at another, priest; at still another, he is transcendent, "appearing above the clouds of the heaven"; at still yet another time he is the just servant, despised, a victim, one put to death, one who by his very death gains a "universal royalty."

At the very outset of his mission, Christ took pains to make it unmistakably clear that he was the "awaited" one. His first appearance among men was simply that of another man, the son of a carpenter. Certainly he was not the first to come before the people and speak to them. Many politico-religious agitators had preceded him, but their success was minimal in the face of the well-established power of the Roman occupation. Christ at once took up his position outside the political arena. As a result of his early public utterances, he was respected as a new prophet (one speaking in the name of Yahweh), one who would complement the teachings of earlier prophets. Yet, as Christ continued his preaching mission, there were more and more efforts on his part to change men's thinking regarding themselves. In fact, at times he showed what can almost be called an aloof transcendence. By certain expressions he identified himself even with Yahweh, while, at the same time, he portrayed himself as a special kind of "only son." This is the very claim which will subsequently fan the wrathful flames of the traditionalists—priests, leaders of the sacerdotal caste, men of law, the Pharisees—and will bring about Christ's eventual trial and death sentence for blasphemy.

Before his death, however, Christ spoke in a mysterious way to the small group of those who had committed themselves to him in full faith (John 16). He spoke of a "third" who was going to come after him, but who could not come until Christ himself had departed, until he had put distance—separation—between himself and his adherents. This would be a *Third* whom his Father and he would send, and who would finish the task of making all thing clear.

The outcome of all this is that Yahweh—that God who, from the time of Abraham, had revealed himself in stages—is, indeed, *One*, but is also, in himself, *three*. And, as St. John sums it up in a perfectly clear and simple statement, "God is love."

The positive exposition of what is generally called the trinitarian mystery is the crowning achievement of God's self-communication during the course of Judaeo-Christian revelation. And it becomes the real stumbling block, the threshold which many will not cross. Judaism, in renouncing Christ as God, is at one with Islamism in its steadfast return to the primitive "bloc" of monotheism.

This attitude, furthermore, is somewhat contradictory.

Without being aware of it at all, these fierce advocates of transcendence are the very ones who cut this transcendence down to an everyday size, the result being that it is not transcendence at all. To the primitive oriental peoples who lived some two thousand years before our own time, belief in but a single God, a being absolutely "other" and impenetrable in itself offered a serious difficulty. Only one small tribe, with the help of Abraham, succeeded in overcoming this difficulty—a tribe later to become the Hebrew nation.

To expect acceptance, however, of this One being—at the same time three—was almost asking too much. Infinitely more difficult, this whole notion was wholly beyond apprehension by the human mind. All those who had been firmly grounded in the original notion of transcendence were unaware that, actually, they were coming back quite docilely to the point of reducing Yahweh to a kind of magical power, to something like a far-away, all embracing Baal. They brushed aside the absolute transcendence of the trinitarian revelation, and, as in the beginning, so now only a small group accepted this teaching, and for the sole reason that they had heard Christ and believed in him.

The trinitarian viewpoint alone establishes a place for the real transcendence—separation, absolute distance—laid down by Yahweh from the very beginning as the principle of the relationship to himself. That God is love is the leading idea of the whole of Revelation, right from the very beginning of the Old Testament. God cannot be love, however, unless he is, *in himself*, relation-to-the-other. Love is an interpersonal relation. If God is "alone in himself," the other term of the relation is man. It may not seem so at first glance, but such a condition would do away with all distance, would be tantamount to anthropomorphizing God or deifying man. If there is to be loyalty to the real idea of transcendence, introduced at the very beginning of Revelation, then there must be acceptance of the concept of the One in Three, a notion impossible of comprehension and one which introduces a language difficulty that is decidedly permanent and embarrassing. Man no longer has words that fit; no longer can he "hem in" God in the way he once could when God was all alone, so to speak; every possible word about God is unavoidably and dreadfully beside the point, and it can never really meet the need.

The long and arduous work involved in the first great councils of the Church (Ephesus, Nicea, and Constantinople) is ample proof that men were profoundly aware of their fundamental and utter powerlessness to express this One in Three. At the same time, however, this recognition resulted in a struggle and a notable advance in thinking with the object of expressing this trinitarian transcendence in such a way that, positively, it be approachable and, negatively, that it not be emptied of its content. Philosophy's efforts to understand more clearly just what is *person* and what is *nature* may be

dated from this time. It is no surprise, either, that Islam shows no trace of this development.

Finally, the Church stopped with the utterance of an official pronouncement—a definition: the divine *Persons* are "subsistent relations." In our turn, then, and at the risk of failure because language is wholly inadequate, we say that God is really transcendent, completely at a distance from man, and is, in himself, the "absolute world of the living relation," One in Three.

It is not pointless to intervene here with a most essential aspect of modern psychology. A comparison suggests itself at this point.

Before a child arrives at his first stage of emotional balance and makes his entrance into the world, the Oedipus crisis must first be settled. By going beyond an exclusive, or predominant, relation to the parent of the opposite sex—a relation which has now become insufficient—the child enters upon a relationship with both parents whereby he is able to take his place as a person distinct and sexed like the parent of the same sex. This parent has now taken his place, so to speak, in the relation-universe of the child with its symbolic meaning. This is the course of identification.

There is general agreement in saying, in technical terms, that the child should move normally from a "dual relation" to the "triangular situation." From that point on, the child has definitely taken his place; the hidden, emotional evolution of this first breaking-out of himself is at an end. What will ensue in the forward motion of

his life will only make explicit and give expression to the personality developed in its dynamic foundations.

If the child is to arrive at a normal, well-balanced state, it must successfully assume its position in a "relation involving three persons." In the same way, the couple finds its natural outlet in the child, its own natural "third dimension." This third dimension is the living, the most specific relation proper to the father and mother, so that a couple which systematically excludes the child is not a normal married couple. Properly speaking, they are no longer really even a *couple* so much as the mere association of two immature, neurotic, badly sexed persons who have found a kind of *modus vivendi*, satisfying for good or for ill, which it often less stable than it appears. By contrast, a normal couple, incapable of having a child, suffers deeply from this lack of its third dimension. It is not impossible, however, given the recognition of this lack and the furtherance of the dialogue, that the child, present by its very absence, will become the paradoxical "third dimension" which brings the marriage unity to completion. In order, therefore, that human personality develop and afterwards become as perfect as it ought, it must successfully find its place in a world in which three persons are related. This is no mere chance happening.

Here we touch upon a rather tender subject. Some authors violently cast aside the very idea of possibly discovering an analogy—in the technical meaning of this word—between the sexed structure of the living and

human world, on the one hand, and the trinitarian mystery on the other. This, doubtless, is linked up with that hovering, formless taboo which modern psychology finds so very difficult to dispel. Fear—or anguish—still exerts the strongest influence on the mystery. According to Thomas Aquinas, for example, the true mystery—especially one that is properly Christian—should have no connection with such disturbing emotions. If the tendency of modern psychology is to put its finger on this fear and then remove it, then it will allow for a more positive grasp of the mystery as such.

No matter how intense the debates, how strong the efforts to ignore it, how towering the evidence marshalled, the trinity as a fact is here to stay. On the one hand, God reveals himself as One in Three; on the other hand, sexuality is seen, in the light of modern psychology, as a relational world which reaches the development it should only when three relations are involved; finally, there is that striking text of Genesis 1:27: "God created man in his image. In the image of God he created him. Male and female he created them."

What impropriety could possibly be found in saying that sexuality as such—the mystery of relation—is an integrating aspect of that "likeness" of himself which God gives to his spiritual creature? The sexed makeup is the living creature's fundamental way of being which, on the human level, expands in the transcendence of consciousness. To ignore this truth or to deny that it can have some kind of connection with the mystery of God would seem to be a kind of blasphemy. Positively, it would amount to the implication that sexuality would be the work of "the spirit of evil."

"And God saw that it was good."

Precisely because it was made "like unto" the infinite dynamism of the relation which is God himself, One and Three, the human race was itself also created in a "rhythmic pattern of three," as modern science has clearly brought out. Two *persons* approach each other; they are "but one flesh" (Genesis 2:24); and their unity gives rise to the third personal dimension, the child—"the other who goes out from them."

Implied in the objection against discerning the analogy between sexuality, as such, and the trinitarian mystery is an objection to all knowledge as certain knowledge. For, on the one hand, the data of science are rendered questionable as testimony; on the other, every "theology" must reduce the living God of revelation to an abstract philosophical principle, one without any concern for human anxiety.

Meaning of the Couple in Revelation

In biblical revelation it is very obvious that God is not sexed. On this precise point the Judaeo-Christian heritage departs from all the mythical religions. At the very be-

ginning of Revelation, Yahweh shows himself as *unique*.
This true God has nothing in common with those ancient,
proliferating god-families with their mother-goddesses
and father-gods. To be sexed belongs only to the creature; God is infiinitely beyond that. We encounter here
again the initial idea of transcendence.

Before the living and transcendent God took discernible place in human history to teach and explain his
"Trinity," Revelation through the prophets had undergone a long and gradual development. Speaking, of
course, in a purely relative way, one is tempted to remark that God allowed centuries to pass before entrust-
ing man with the truth that he is not only One, but
also One in Three, the reason for this delay in Revelation being that man might be prone to fall back to the
myth-level of sexed gods.

With the revelation of the Trinity, sexuality is cast into
a brand new light, seen now as enjoying a divine security. Sexuality is now known as a positive good, described
even as a "likeness." But just that: *likeness,* not identity.
Analogical reflection, an essential vestige, a starting point
as it were, of an absolutely transcendent, relational reality not yet unfolded. Starting with this "break-through,"
with this root distinction, biblical Revelation will cast
light on the human couple—that is, on the true meaning of sexuality.

First of all, sexuality is proposed as the very foundation of living nature and of human nature. So clearly

does biblical revelation make this point, and from the very outset of Genesis, that there is no need to dwell on it here.

All this is contained in the word "likeness." One is almost tempted to say that the vocation of the human race is to start with being tried by its division and searching in order eventually to discover its unity. On the other hand, after indicating his withdrawal behind absolute transcendence, God will devote the whole period of the Old Testament to going in the opposite direction, disclosing that, although only One, He is divided into Three Persons.

The starting point of the world, as God sees it, is said to be this relation of the couple, of man and woman. In what followed, this relation was called upon to adopt a quite different and, at first sight, a quite extraordinary meaning.

The main topic of Revelation is that of the dramatic split between man and God (Genesis 3) and of the reconciliation in the "alliance" which God made with man for his eventual salvation. This is the light which the Word of God gave to the drama of history: birth, the uncertain wavering of time, death, and resurrection.

With Abraham, first of all, this essential topic of the "alliance" is voiced in a "style" that smacks of magic to some extent. With Moses, it takes on a more juridical look. And suddenly, with the prophetic outlook, another form of expression comes to light, and that is the ultimate one. The allegory most capable of expressing the dramatic dialogue of God with humanity is that of the dramatic human couple. The lived-experience of sexuality, even in its very twofold tension, is the way of approach to the mystery of the alliance. Marriage, the drama of the infidelity of the Bride and the infinite faithfulness of the Bridegroom who, through the proving-ground of the desert, finally arouses in the Bride a faithfulness of reply, then establishes a definitive "marriage." Such, in summary, is humanity's history: God is this infinitely faithful Bridegroom whose all-powerful love eventually elevates the Bride's defective love to his own level.

This central theme was first introduced by the prophet Hosea, taken up by Isaias, Ezechiel, the *Song of Songs*, and by many passages in the Psalms or Prophets.

The Hebrew word *hesed* in Hosea means the attitude of love in which God (the Bridegroom) takes the initiative. The word has a meaning whose complex richness has been brought out so well by exegetes that no single modern word can express its full content. Faithfulness, love, tenderness. The striking thing is that, by way of the Greek (and, later, Latin) traditions, the Hebrew word finally comes to be expressed by "grace." It would seem that this should urge theologians not to forget, as an essential starting point of their treatment of grace and in line with Sacred Scripture, that there is a question, *first of all*, of an "interpersonal relation."

The development of this theme of the "dramatic couple" comes to a peak in St. Paul who frequently

and explicitly in his letters speaks of the marriage of
Christ and his Church, thus elevating human marriage
to the status of being an image of the Christ-Church
marriage.

It must be remembered that this theme finds its
development around the love of the couple as such.
While the offspring is not absent, it still remains half-
hidden in the background. Paramount is the love of the
couple, namely, the "first movement" of sexuality.

In the light of this central biblical theme, sexuality
can be said to be, in the Judaeo-Christian Revelation, not
only the foundation of the created world, but it is also,
for the human race, the place of opposing tensions
where the race becomes conscious of its destiny: a call
to the infinite, a "slipping backwards," drama, and the
certitude of transcendent "restoration" by the "grace" of
God.

One final observation, of an altogether different kind,
is called for here.

According to the established teaching of the Church,
in order that a marriage be valid—and henceforth indissoluble[1]—it is necessary and sufficient that the con-
tracting parties be capable of sexual relations. Sterility—

---

[1] "Indissoluble"—namely, intrinsically, by the married partners
themselves. A valid marriage, but one not yet consummated, can be
dissolved by the Holy See (for a serious reason) and by Church
law (cf. *Code of Canon Law,* can. 1119), repeating the teaching of
the Council of Trent that a valid marriage, but one not consummated, is dissolved by the religious profession (solemn) of one or
both married partners.

the *impotentia generandi* of the canonists—is not an impediment to marriage. Sexual impotence, of whatever kind it may be—*impotentia coeundi*—is an absolute impediment to marriage when it is a condition prior to the marriage, absolute and perpetual.

Furthermore, normal spouses—those capable of effecting pregnancy—who would by prior agreement exclude all conception, would not contract a valid marriage. The "contract" is null and void.

To bring these observations together is very illuminating. Although it is true that sexuality is destined for conception, in the eyes of the Church (at least implicitly) it is the sexual expression of love between man and woman, and this is foundation enough for establishing a married couple. The truth is that this expression of love, looked upon in itself and independently of conception, has a deep meaning, a coherence which acts as a condition for the reality of the sacrament.

Shadows

In one whole line of development in Revelation, human sexuality is shown in a decidedly positive light. But, *at the same time,* Revelation depicts the deficiencies, the contradictions, and the tragedies attendant upon sexuality. Not always through its pages does sexuality reach its full meaning as at the beginning of Genesis. Moreover, Revelation provides the scene for abnormal, even incoherent behavior-patterns for which man can find no cure for the reason that something is operative which curbs, blocks, and irremediably separates man from the approach to the fullness of the lived-relation.

The Old Testament recounts many instances of these tragedies of human sexuality, always in connection—explicit or not—with the drama of the "dialogue with Yahweh" as expressed in the allegory of the Bridegroom and Bride.

Barrenness (an apparent sign of a divine "curse"), the tragedy of polygamy or legal concubinage, jealousies which lead to murder, adulteries, prostitution, the thousand and one forms of the "uncontrolled sexual" exploding in catastrophe, the horror of sexual perversions—all these are to be found in the different historical accounts of the Bible. On reflection, nothing is so striking as this contrast: on the one hand, through Revelation a people grasps the ideal meaning of human sexuality; on the other, the sacred authors outdo themselves in showing how far, actually and inexcusably, the people depart from this ideal.

Love and Death

By way of parentheses, Revelation did not have to give heed to the ongoing and impossible-to-resolve debate between love and death.

In the ancient oriental way of thinking, there is no clear awareness of the specific and somewhat absolute value of the individual person. Its mentality was, above all, tribal. In other words, in the eyes of the Jew of Solomon's time, what really mattered was the lot of the "chosen people": its sufferings, its victories, its failures. But the personal lot of the individual Jews held no real importance distinct from, although bound up with, that of the people as a whole. Twentieth-century people of the western world hardly view this attitude with sympathy, although it does underlie what we call Islamic "fatalism." In the face of a person's death, these ancients never really experienced its full dramatic meaning. However, the solemn declaration by Ezechiel that Yahweh takes an interest in each individual man, followed by the Book of Job, effects a new awareness of the suffering *subject*. But the modern consciousness—when it has the courage (or the strength) to face reality—is well aware of a situation that, though unbearable, cannot be changed. In the love between two people—to the extent that the love is a real relation of two people of sufficient emotional maturity—there is introduced a humanness which transcends time. Into such a love a factor is introduced which resists anything that would compromise or destroy that love. People refer to this element of firm stability each time they say, "Love is forever." And what is the meaning of "forever" in this context? Simply that such factors as aging and dying are put out of mind as having no final significance in the undying character of love. Still, no matter how real the love and its beyond-time stability, death will always come as a harsh interruption of the relation.

In a southern French village this past summer, word reached the bride-to-be that the bridegroom had just been killed in an automobile accident, ten minutes before the time of the wedding ceremony. Although a tragedy like this is certainly enough to cause the deepest anguish, there is something to be learned from the amazement of the young lady's friends that she did not lose her mind.

Curiously, the Old Testament, which makes no spiritual or psychological analysis of the human couple as such, speaks only of the drama of the "allegorical couple." And in that there is no question of death. There is only question of the "proving-ground of the desert" which will make definitive unity possible.

The "Fall"

Something happened to prevent this relation from being lived out in its fullness. What was it?

Revelation offers for our consideration the third chapter of Genesis, undoubtedly the most meaningful, yet most puzzling of all. No rational explanation, I believe, can be found there, one which, like a simple mathematical proof, makes the matter utterly clear. The drama of love is not of the order of reason.

Our everyday language is risky here; it is too easy to adopt expressions of abstract reasoning or of childish description. Too, there is the additional risk of being false to the Church's tradition. Oversimplified textbooks and some abridged catechisms, especially the older ones, are the chief offenders in this regard because they leave the impression that this entire subject can be easily outlined.

Despite every precaution, the risk is not easily avoided. Efforts to delineate what is the very heart of the human drama are handicapped by a vocabulary of relative terms —accurate, yes, but inadequate.

What took place, as narrated in the third chapter of Genesis, is of an entirely different order from that of the morality which governs the individual. In fact, to use the term "sin" here may give the wrong idea. There is no question of a "personal sin" in the events of the third chapter of Genesis, but of a sin of nature. And "nature" here refers to human nature without any special metaphysical preference. Negatively stated, it is not human nature as assumed by each personal ego that is meant.

This original mystery—is it not even more mysterious and yet more original than it is made out to be? The first eleven chapters of Genesis fall under a very particular literary genus. These chapters are not historical as we understand the term, that is, light shed on human history. As for Adam, he is Man; Eve, Woman; at the same time, they are the first couple on whose level—from the evolutionary point of view—the transforming change from life to spirit took place in answer to God's call. The Genesis account employs symbols to explain a more vital and more realistic situation than any language can express. There is question of a first historical, concrete situation and of the couple which founded the human race, so to speak. Next we have the situation of the "split" which is passed on to all humanity, although not by means of a "juridical" solidarity, but through an existential, ontological solidarity. The very effort to discuss this fact makes it necessary to tread an uneasy path between juridical resolution and flights into poetry.

An illustration may help, but no illustration can give any more than a mere suggestion of how to view this matter.

A mother is knitting in the living-room while her three-year-old child is playing on the rug. Suddenly the child sees a wall plug near the door and crawls over to examine it. The mother calls out, "Don't touch that, dear; you'll hurt yourself!" But it never enters her mind to restrain the child from moving around. Quietly, of course, the child goes over to this mysterious and fascinating object and thrusts his fingers into the holes. Shock, fall, panic, screams. The distraught mother rushes to soothe the little fellow.

After this experience, which could have been prevented at the cost of the child's freedom, the child has learned two things in his young life: 1) he can never know everything; 2) his mother loves him even more than he realized.

All in all, the essential point in the biblical account —and which the comparison helps to emphasize—is that *Someone* (God) asks of *someone* (the couple) a particular reply. This request is made under the aspect of a prohibition, much as with the mother and her child. On reflection, this means that the one making the request invites the other to consent to a "gaping void," to consent to a relation to him. "You don't know everything; you can't know everything, for you are not I; trust in me without understanding." This is, literally, a calling to love. As with the child, the couple of chapter three in Genesis will not accept this distance, this "separation," and plans to ignore it. That couple does not truly love. Its inclination is to avoid being present to the Word they hear; they refuse to listen. There, it would seem, is the existential place of pride.

The biblical text shows this very clearly. The couple is tempted to annihilate this distance by paying no attention to the Word: by "eating of the fruit," they will be "as God."

Now there remains the question of the couple as found in the first two chapters of Genesis. The whole sexed human race is contained virtually in this first human couple, so that the couple embraces in itself both the whole of humanity and humanity as individually expressed. This is historical in the fullest sense, and each human being that comes into the world can be said to create anew this action started by the first couple.

The couple is first seen as embodying a certain perfection of unity. Then, as a result of the division in which humanity no longer listens to God (in brief, this is the central mystery of liberty), the couple itself becomes deeply disturbed by what happened. In other words, *by itself* the couple cannot reestablish or bring this unity to fulfillment. When Yahweh came at twilight and questioned Adam about what had happened, Adam replied, "It wasn't I! It was the woman you gave me." Adam thus breaks his solidarity with Eve whom he had described as "flesh of my flesh and bone of my bones."

Up to now we have had two *persons* in Adam and Eve. Now something new is introduced—original sin—and we may look upon it as something which divides and disunites, something which is the logical corollary of the attitude which dismissed the Word of the Other. Original sin introduces the whole disputed problem of suffering into the human reality. The couple—the very substructure of the human race—engages in strife, with ensuing torment in their lives. Here, too, the tension of human sexuality finds explanation. The living universe is as one betrayed by the Being which was entrusted with summing it up within itself and giving answer in humanity's name, and St. Paul will later note that all creation groans in the pains of childbirth.

On account of the resultant new void in human consciousness, man readily understands the second development in Revelation: the Word of Salvation. Only original sin allows the human race to know simultaneously the worthiness of its calling, the deficiencies of human love, and the reality of salvation by the Other. "O happy fault," the liturgy of the paschal night says, "that merited so great a Redeemer."

To give expression to the mystery is not to remove its character of mystery. Accordingly, we may say that there is a strange proneness in the very heart of the human race to cling to what is at hand and thereby to ignore the voice of the Other. There is even a nostalgia for what was not accomplished, and, instead of this nostalgia converting itself into hope, it actually withdraws into itself in an instinctive quest for a present that is rapidly moving into the past. Modern psychology detects a trace of this in the reaction of the very young child which longs to return to the mother's womb. According to Freudian discoveries, this tendency to withdraw is clearly a fact, a normal psychological defense process, but knowing that it is a fact is not the same as explaining it.

This biblical drama finds expression in man's sexual make-up. In fact, man's sexual make-up accounts for the possibility that the drama even began, since it plays the role of at least a basic condition. Returning to the example of the child which wants to find things out for itself and pays no attention to its mother's warning, we shall see a parallel—not perfect, of course—with the drama we are discussing: regarded in its specific relation

of dialogue, it is really the *couple* which dismisses the
word of the Other (God). In a sense, God can be com-
pared to the mother or, better, to the complex parental
insistence which wants to instill in the child that freedom
whereby it will undertake to act on its own initiative.
Literally and factually, however, the human race is not
a child in the presence of the Mystery who is speaking;
it is the unity of two persons who, together, can conceive
and who seek forgetfulness in a display of freedom which
is actually license.

Freedom fettered by itself or by its own bewilderment,
the breaking off of the dialogue, "pride" in the traditional
sense—all these lead to conscious "nakedness," that is, to
loneliness, to weakness, to anguish.

What is called "original sin" is the very mystery of the
human condition in its ambivalence because the fact of
a refusal—forevermore stamped on every individual
human nature—to hear the Word of Him who, in his
revelation of salvation, was destined, step by step, to dis-
close Himself as Love.

The Perishable Nature of Genital Sexuality

In that tribal way of thinking which is peculiar to the
ancient East, the idea of a personal destiny beyond death
was very vague. First of all, it was understood that the

righteous man—the one who lived according to the law of Yahweh—was wealthy, fortunate and longlived. ("He will see his children unto the third and fourth generation" is, strangely enough, still found in the ritual of the nuptial blessing.) Ezechiel's declaration of the worth of the individual and the sorrowful musings of Job were invaluable for understanding that suffering and death were not a personal *punishment*, but a mystery. Only later, in the Greek era with the Machabees, was there detected in Revelation the notion of a full after-death destiny.

This idea of a personal resurrection was by no means universal in Christ's time. One Gospel event in particular is quite explicit in this regard: the conversation of Jesus with the Sadducees.

The Sadducees were rich men, cynical in their outlook, who were opposed to this whole idea of resurrection, a fairly common theme in Christ's preaching. They went out of their way to trap him and to humiliate him. Strikingly enough, their questions were based on a sexual situation. St. Luke (20:27–38) tells the story.

Now there came to him certain of the Sadducees, who say that there is no resurrection, and they questioned him, saying, "Master, Moses has written for us: 'If a man's brother die, having a wife, and he be childless, his brother will take the widow and raise up issue to his brother.' Now there were seven brothers. And the first took a wife and died childless.

And the next took her, and he also died childless.
And the next took her, and he also died childless. Then the third took her; and in like manner
all seven, and they died without leaving children.
Last of all, the woman also died. At the resurrection,
therefore, of which of them will she be wife? For
the seven had her as wife."

And Jesus said to them, "The children of this
world marry and are given in marriage. But those
who shall be accounted of that world and of the
resurrection from the dead neither marry nor take
wives. *For neither shall they be able to die any
more*, for they are equal to the angels, and are sons
of God, being sons of the resurrection."

It follows from this that, in Christ's way of thinking,
sexuality, in its genital expression, belongs to time, yet
its transitoriness in no way diminishes its positive nature.
The relation of love, in the world of the resurrection,
assumes a place superior to the genital expression of sexuality. And the text carries this strange declaration of a
link between genital sexuality and death: "For neither
shall they be able to die any more."

We have seen that, at one and the same time, the
genital expression of sexuality is creative of life and revealer of individual death, and that beyond time it has
no meaning. It tends toward full realization beyond time,
yet it never arrives.

In the world of the resurrection—freed from time, in that it shares in the eternal fullness of God's being—sexuality, therefore, is clearly a thing of the past. Begetting children no longer has any meaning since humanity has reached the perfection of its growth. And sexual love, a preparatory stage connected with procreation, has itself crossed over into a literally inexpressible love, sharing in the trinitarian transcendence. Clearly, the Sadducees were unprepared for such understanding.

This passage of genital sexuality from time into a relation of a transcendental order, as a result of God's participation in human history, is made uniquely clear in another part of Revelation.

There lived quietly in Israel a young girl by the name of Mary. Like every young girl brought up on the teachings of Sacred Scripture, she awaited the coming of the Messiah. There was urgency in the way he was awaited, and Mary, as likely was true of her girl companions, hoped and longed for the incomparable honor of being his mother—much as Samuel's mother had dreamed.

Judging from evidence offered in the gospels, Mary had nothing outstanding to commend her. Since it is not even mentioned, it seems safe to say that her own birth took place under the most ordinary circumstances. She was the result of human sexuality, fruit of the sexual relations of a man and woman—her mother and father (the historical names ascribed to them, from this point of view, is of little moment).

In the beginning of St. Luke's Gospel, Mary appears to have enjoyed a unique freedom for the reason that, unlike the "prototype couple," nothing restrained Mary in the dialogue to which God invited her. She is complete attention, ready for everything, entirely agreeable, never asking for explanations. This is a bewildering, almost miraculous state of affairs: she is like a child who would continue as a child, yet would be mature enough to do exactly what its mother said and to pay no attention to the wall-plug.

From the annunciation, St. Luke goes on, Mary learned that she was perfect in *hesed* (the expression "full of grace," in the usual translation, falls far short of the meaning). According to the Greek word, *checharitomē*, as used by Luke, and taken in conjunction with Hosea 2, Mary is she in whom is realized the fullness of this "love, tenderness, faithfulness of Yahweh" which is expressed in *hesed.* In Mary is realized that "definitive marriage" proclaimed between the infinitely faithful Bridegroom and the Bride finally willing to consent without reservation.

She is with child.

She is with child by God.

She is with child to such a degree that Joseph, her fiancé (whom she did not yet "know"), was completely upset and, because he did not know what had happened, of a mind to put her away secretly. But Joseph learned in time, and he assumed the role of human father in the case of this unquestionably unique Child—the living, visible Mystery.

And Mary is a virgin "before, during, and after," according to the traditional expression. This means that in the life of this couple—who are a kind of new "prototype"—genital sexuality no longer has any meaning, since *God is there* with them.

The historical reality of Christ, "the incarnate Word," transforms this situation to that very point where genital sexuality—and even in time—passes over to the mode of the world's transcendent relation to the Resurrection.

Whether this be accepted or not on faith—something entirely different from accepting scientific findings—the fact is that this is the content of Revelation regarding sexuality.

In an effort to state this succinctly, it can be said that there is a distinction to be made between "ontological sexuality"—the irreversible basis of the lived relation for created being—and its genital expression which, since it is of time, is necessarily ambivalent.

Light

Illumination is thrown on the inexplicable, insoluble ambivalence of sexuality, as it appears to modern psychology and anthropology, when these perspectives are admitted. And, unquestionably, the light which is needed has its source only in these perspectives.

However, a question remains regarding perspectives which are not of the intellectual and philosophical order, but of the order of *encounter*. This is not *demonstrable* any more than love in its sexual expression is *demonstrated*. It is possible only to make an effort to present, in more or less renewed terms, the meaning of what has been told us.

Each one of us derives from sexuality the basic condition of life. The first stage begins its course—a mysterious, primitive, yet careful production—in the secrecy of the mother's womb. The extraordinary biological activity of embryogenesis results in what is really the threshold of the first uterine contractions and the breaking of the amniotic sac. But we already exist, we are virtually ourselves, and that without our being aware of it. We are thought of, spoken of, given a name (in fact two names, because it is not yet known whether we are a boy or a girl); people form pictures of us; we are already quite important and, from the legal point of view, we are already a subject capable of inheriting.

Vague and skimpy though this knowledge is, it does, nonetheless, exist. We are not just little animals. And there is no exaggeration in saying that, with the unfathomable "gift" of heredity and its initial constitution in reality, our particular personality has already vaguely begun *its* own history.

This first phase is already ambivalent. There is the irresistible force that "pushes us out" and there is also this "comfort" for which, later on, there will be that "nostalgia," that "homesickness" disclosed in the findings of modern psychology.

Suddenly everything breaks loose. An indescribable rending results. Our first home is split from top to bottom, and we are cast out, without hope of return, from our first existential experience.

Our birth is truly an inexpressible uprooting, but without it growth cannot take place. And we go into the world, man or woman potentially, springing from the sex of our mother, brought into being by the sex of our father.

A first level of self-realization is possible at this stage. We are going to take our place as a subject in the relations established throughout an evolution which is never really completed, and we shall assume that place in alternating successes and failures, joys and suffering. Nothing, clearly, is resolved or settled. Our inner contradiction —and sexuality is the focal point where awareness of this is centered—is simultaneously both more fundamental and more personal than can ever be expressed. We are in the "time-uterus," fettered both by the "will to live" and by the "desire to remain at rest" which are, in this respect, incompatible.

But the existent Love—the One in Three—does not allow this fettered freedom to remain stagnant. He inserts himself into time, into the sexual condition, and, thereby, he points out its relativity.

And now the second rupture is disclosed. Like the sac of waters, time is torn from top to bottom. We are cast out—but this time in full consciousness of the drama— toward a world which we have never previously experienced except for realizing our successful relations, and with all that inevitable ambivalence which reveals both promise and dissatisfaction. We know of this world into which we may enter by that second delivery which is death "in Christ arising," only because Christ has told us that it is the kingdom of perfect love *beyond time*.

It is just as impossible for us to form the least idea of this world as it is impossible for the fetus, after eight and a half months, to have the slightest idea of where he is going. This man—who I was already at that time, ready to utter my first cry of both suffering and of "welcome"— was unable to form a picture of himself in any way approaching the picture which his mother (in whom he existed) or his father (who had put him there) had formed.

Has sufficient thought ever been given to this, that if the fetus did have a clear, developed consciousness, it might not survive the last moments in the uterus as anything but life's final moments? Or, if it were really conscious at such times, would it not perhaps experience the preparation for its birth as preparation for the end of life it had been leading—in other words, as preparation for its own death?

Sin

The history of man in its entirety—that of the race as well as that of each person—appears to us, then, as a real dialogue with the Living Love, finally triumphant, whose ontological sexuality and its expression in time allow us to grasp both existence and absolute transcendence.

In this light, moral uneasiness takes on a completely new meaning. Culpability—a human experience as fundamental as the sexual experience with which it is necessarily linked—turns toward penance, that is, toward a call which is *certain to be heard*. Such, indeed, is the meaning of the dramatic dialogue between the thief and Christ on Calvary.

Sin, therefore, is a concept of the *religious* order, and not only of the moral order. It is not in reference to a law, first of all, that sin has a fixed place, but in relation to God of whom the law is a first expression, directed toward making us conscious of the meaning of our liberty *and* of our insufficiency.

In conclusion, there are certain considerations to be emphasized here.

Sin, according to the first three chapters of Genesis, is the attitude of the human race which, in its ontological sexed makeup, limits itself to self and stops hearing the *Other who Speaks*.

There is nothing astonishing in the fact that, throughout the whole course of Scripture, sin—collective and personal—is looked upon as being, essentially, *idolatry*. By turning a deaf ear to God who speaks outside of time, the human race, collectively and individually, *on infinitely variable levels of consciousness,* is going to spend its time in the search for "false gods" in time. The most fascinating, to be sure, will be sexuality itself, not in its erotic aspect, as is too often believed, but in its inexhaustible mystery. And, as a way of expression, it will be in the foreground. The Israelitic nation, deserting Yahweh to devote itself to the worship of various divinities of the surrounding country, is pictured by Hosea and Ezechiel as the unfaithful Bride who prostitutes herself to successive lovers, abandoning the unchangeable love of her true Bridegroom.

When St. Paul addresses the nascent Christian communities of the first century, he astonishes no one when he explicitly likens some forms of behavior—sexual or otherwise—to that of idolatry, for the reason that it is not "compatible with the Kingdom of God." Paul's correspondents were of a mentality which, in many respects, was still primitive, still heavily influenced by the various cults in which sexuality, under different forms, had a dominant role. Paul's task was to make his readers understand that the sexual act and its attendant ecstasy (even with temple prostitutes of either sex) was not a religious act directed toward the *true* transcendent God; it was no more a religious act than exhibitions of power or riches. Sexual fecundity itself, a reply to God's call, is not even the final term of our destiny. In a sense, virginity, even in time, excels the genital expression of sexuality. Every sin, therefore, is idolatry. In itself, then, sin is the diminishing or denying of love since the true God is the absolute "Relation to the Other." In Christ's words, the only attitude that puts us in agreement with God is love, namely, living all our intersubjective relations in such a way that the other, howsoever diverse, with whom we have to deal—whether in a passing or lasting way—may be experienced as a *subject* and not as *object* or as holder of the object which is adored.

This idolatry, however, unfolds on very different levels. It may, without question, be an idolatry of which we are conscious and upon which we have reflected. Most often it is instinctive, so to speak, not an idolatry to which we have deliberately succumbed. Quite often, also, it is unconscious and escapes prior control.

The Christian man, St. John says, "does not sin," that is to say, he recognizes Christ as God and Savior from whom he expects everything. St. Paul says, however, "I do the evil which I will not, and I do not the good which I will. And if I do the evil which I will not, it is not I who does it; it is sin which does it in me." A startling statement, at first glance, but one which expresses the full drama of the Christian man. Against his most refined choice, against his most personal clinging to God, his true love, man idolizes some other object in the dim regions of himself. This unbearable division within him is what alone allows man, in the last analysis, to realize, once and for all, the salvation which Christ works out in him.

From the moral point of view, in the light of Revelation, sexuality can no longer be experienced under the guise of magic anguish, but rather in the positive mean-

ing of a drama flowing out into the transcendent fulfillment of love.

In times far past, thunder was thought of as divine;
epilepsy as the presence of an evil spirit. Step by step,
science has enlightened the mind of man with the causes
of confusion. In the same way, sexuality and the pleasures
it gives have been made out as god or devil. Will modern
science, at last, enable us to put sexuality in its proper
place, that is, in relation to the mystery of the Living God
who is above and beyond all that exists?